The Narrative Unity of the Cursor Mundy

Ernest G. Mardon
Edited by Claire MacMaster

Golden Meteorite Press

A Golden Meteorite Press Book.

© 2012 copyright Printed in Canada by Golden Meteorite Press. No part of this publication may be reproduced, stored in a retrieval system or transmit- ted, in any form or by any means, without prior written consent of the publisher or a licence from The Canadian Copyright Licensing Agency (Access Copyright).
For an Access Copyright licence, visit www.accesscopyright.ca Or call toll free number: 1-800-893- 5777.

Cover design and Typeset by Bianca Ho
Edited by Claire MacMaster

Published by Golden Meteorite Press.
126 Kingsway Garden, Post Office Box 34181
Edmonton, Alberta, CANADA. T5G 3G4
Telephone: 1-(780)-378-0063
Email: aamardon@yahoo.ca
Website: www.austinmardon.org

Library and Archives Canada Cataloguing in Publication

Mardon, Ernest G., 1928-
    The narrative unity of the Cursor mundi / Ernest G. Mardon & Austin A. Mardon ; edited by Claire MacMaster.

ISBN 978-1-897472-57-6

1. Cursor mundi. I. Mardon, Austin A. (Austin Albert)
II. MacMaster, Claire III. Title.

PR1966.M37 2012   821'.1   C2012-905521-2

Dedicated to Marie Mardon

Contents

Introduction..6

Chapter I..12

Chapter II...28

    Medieval Concept of History....................41

Chapter III..43

Chapter IV..54

Chapter V...86

Chapter VI...103

Chapter VII..125

Chapter VIII...137

Chapter IX...154

Notes..156

Acknowledgements.......................................191

Introduction

While the exiled Dante was penning the "Divine Comedy" in Italy, an unknown clerk was writing in the south of Scotland the "Cursor Mundi", which is double the length of "Paradise Lost", and is one of the most remarkable pieces of literature that survives from the Medieval period. This poem, drawn from Biblical paraphrases, ancient Christian myth, medieval legends, lives of the saints and a mass of miscellaneous information, appears in some ten manuscripts which vary in length from fragments of a few hundred lines to the complete work of some twenty-five thousand lines.

The Northern origin of the "Cursor Mundi" is indicated by the poet himself in reference to the section on the Assumption of the Virgin Mary, which he recast into the northern dialect of Middle English:

> In suthrin englijs was it draun,
> And i haue turned it till vr aun
> Langage of þe norþren lede,
> Þat can nan oþer englis rede.

The precise provenance of the original "Cursor Mundi" has been the subject of speculation by scholars (2) for the past hundred years. Stated opinions are rather evenly divided between the lowlands of Scotland, and one of the northern countries of England, usually Durham. (3)

Much of the difficulty arises from vagueness on the part of the sholars regarding the particular manuscript referred to. It is essential to maintain a distinction between a lost original manuscript, regarding which only inferences are possible, and certain manuscripts that have been preserved to the present. Apparently those favouring Durham have reference to the Cotton manuscript rather than to the lost original. Before a decision on the locality is reached, one has to account for the somewhat ambiguous passage in the Prologue of the "Cursor Mundi":

Efter hali kirkes state	
Þis ilke boke es translate,	232
vnto engliss tung to rede	
For þe luue englijs lede,	
Englis lede of meri ingeland	
For þe comen to vnþerstand.	236
Frenkis rimes here i rede	
Comunlu in illka stede;	
Þat es most made for frankis men,	
Quat helpis him þat non can cen.	240
Of ingland þe nacione	
Er englijs men in commune,	
Þe speche þat men may mast wid spede	
Mast to speke þar-wid war nede;	244
Seldom was for ani chance	
Englis tong preched in france,	
Gif we þaim ilkan þair language,	
And þan de we na vtetrage.	248
To leuid and englis men i spell	
Þat understandis quat i can tell,	

Here England is mentioned specifically. For this reason several scholars, in particular Strandberg, reject Scotland: I should like to assume, like Kaluza, that the original was written in Scotland, if it were not for a passage that seems to speak against this." (5) As a kind of compromise, he suggests Northumberland. Actually, it is the contrast between "Inglis" and "Frankus" that concerns the Cursor poet. Emerson remarks:

> Lowland Scoth, as it is called, is an outgrowth of Northern English, and did not differ from it materially until about 1450. In this early period the language of the Scottish writers and that of "Cursor Mundi" or other Northern works is almost, if not quite. Identical. Moreover, the Scots themselves called the language English, or Inglis, their form of the word. (6)

Emerson demonstrates that the term "Scottish" was not commonly used until the end of the fifteenth century, hence "English" at the time was applied to all localities where non-Gaelic or non-French was spoken, including Southern Scotland. Textual support is found at line 24, 765 where William the Conquerer is referred to as "William bastard". Other versions of the legend of the establishment of the feast of Our Lady's Conception refer to King Wiliam in a more respectful manner. (7)

The time of composition of the "Cursor Mundi" is also subject to some dispute. The first attempt to assign a date was made by Murray, "...written, near Durham, about 1275-1300 (while Alexander III reigned in Scotland), and preserved in an orthography not much later." (8) Murray's dating rest on the Cotton manuscript Vespasian A III, which in any case is younger than he supposed. (9) His date is probably a guess. Hupé fixes the time at 1245-90. (10) The earlier date he deduces from a reference in line 9515 to "sent Robert bok", that is Robert Grosseteste's (11) "Château d'Amour".

The terminal date is assigned on negative evidence: no

mention is made of the explusion from England of the "felun iuus" in the year 1290, and no mention is made either of a "groat", a new silver coin minted in 1279. Actually Hupé has settled on his date to agree with his preconceptions regarding the author of the "Cursor Mundi." Strandberg says, without elaboration, "it was composed just before 1300." (12) The latest date for the writing of this poem is 1320, and is given by Jakob Schipper. (13) It appears probably, however, that the "Cursor Mundi" original was composed in the southern part of Scotland at about 1399. It is neither possible nor necessary to locate or date it more precisely.

This vast religious epic, which describes the history of salvation, is unquestionably the work of a single resourceful poet who drew liberally from a variety of English, French and Latin sources. (14) He may also have added several thousand lines on the original poem which he outlines on the original poem which he outlines in the Prologue. (15) The poet makes few personal references to himself in his long work. Two of the most significant indicate that he was a priest. (16)

Surviving in one or more editions is the complete "Cursor Mundi" as projected in the Prologue by the author. The poet ordinarily wrote in "short meter", that is, a pair of rhymed lines having four alternating accents of each. There are also 1031 lines in a "langer bastune", that is, a line of seven accents in rhymed groups of four or more lines. These begin at line 14, 937. At line 23, 944 begin 135 stanzas of "rime couée".

The large number of manuscripts that have survived the destruction of the monasteries and years of wanton neglect evidences the great popularity of the "Cursor Mundi". A total of ten complete or fragmentary manuscripts are extant. (17) Richard Morris late in the last century edited four of these manuscripts, in parallel columns, for The Early English Text Society. (18) In this work, we will use the Göttingen manuscript Theol. 107. This manuscript is the most important and most representative of the surviving copies of the "Cursor Mundi".

It and the Cotton manuscript sometimes differ in phrasing, but such differnces, chiefly lexical, are most pronounced in the first part of Göttingen manuscript preceding a transition first noted by Barth. (19) This occurs at approximately line 10, 962. (20) Beyond this rift the Göttingen manusciript and the Cotton manuscript, the two are almost identical. The Göttingen manuscript ends at line 27, 566, in the sixth of the so-called "Aditions". The relationship between the several manuscripts is of some interest, chiefly as a guide to comparing various readings. This, however, lies outside of the scope of this work.

The "Cursor Mundi" recounts the history of the world from Creation to the Last Judgement. This work, however, is not a rambling collection of stories, myths and legends as one might judge from the title "Cursor Mundi", (Surveyor of the World) but a highly organized account of man's existence and his destiny in this world. The hand of God is present throughout the poem, in the same way as we see it in the illustrations of Medieval Manuscripts. (21)

Our purpose is to show the artistic unity of this long poem that deals with human salvation. The poet binds the various elements of his narrative together by his skillful use of prophecy, and the blending in of such legends as the Oil of Mercy, and the history of the Roodtree. The whole monumental work is framed in the contemporary Medieval devotion to Our Blessed Lady.

The unknown author of the "Cursor Mundi" was writing in a tstrong tradition; he had before him many examples of works on the history of salvation in both Latin and the vernacular. He had also many paraphrases of the Old and New Testaments, along with the collections of myths, legends and the apocryphal Gospels. Nevertheless, his work is unique because it is the most comprehensive poetical treatment of all the important events in the religious history of the world written in the vernacular during the late Middle Ages. It is also unique in being the first long complete poem on a religious topic written after the Norman Conquest in the English language. (22) The art of the Cursor poet, we intend to demonstrate in this work, lies in the manner in which he selected his sources, and his blending of these sources into a smooth poetical narrative in such a way that the reader is carried along by the exciting story of man's fall and redemption. The "Cursor Mundi" is a tightly constructed work of art, with clarity of purpose, a clear principle of unity, and is progressive towards a goal. The aim of this work is to show how the poet creates an organic whole from the combining of the various sources Latin, English and French. It will be shown that the significant Medieval poem is bound together by three unifying strands:

1) The work is framed in the devotion to Our Lady
2) The thread of redemption is traced through the history of the wands that became the wood of the cross and,
3) Through the myth of the search for the Oil of Mercy.

Before examining what the poet says his aims are in the Prologue, we shall endeavor to place the "Cursor Mundi" in its spiritual and intellectual milieu.

Chapter I

As the "Cursor Mundi" is a long narrative poem, which deals not only with religious matters but also with historical matter, we are to consider first the medieval approach to history, and second the religious and spiritual climate of the century in which the "Cursor Mundi" was written.

Let us first then have a look at Medieval man's view of history:

a) **Medieval Concept of History**

It has often been pointed out that the Christianity of Medieval historians induced them to look at the past in terms of God's purpose for the whole of mankind, and this universalizing tendency led many writers in England as well as elsewhere to start their works with the creation of the world. These works then went on to describe the creation of Adam and his fall, and to outline the manner in which the various nations had arisen in the course of time. The author of the "Cursor Mundi" wrote in the tradition of Medieval historians and chroniclers. He attempts to satisfy his readers' desire for a better knowledge of sacred history.

Universal history, of which the "Cursor Mundi" is an outstanding poetical example, arose within the Judeo-Christian tradition where God was the God of all peoples. (1) Medieval history was universal because it was the record of the acts of God in the human story. The Biblical conception of time is not a cyclical one, based on the periodic renewal of events, as with the Greeks and the Romans, but a linear one, made up of a succession of once-and-for-all actions directed towards the final goal of history. (2) The centre of both the revelation and fulfillment of the plan of human salvation is Christ. The general framework of the divine plan was well known to Medieval man. The major stages of history, which commenced with the creation and fall, reach their climax with the redeeming incarnation and end with the second coming of the Lord, were included in most religious histories of salvation during the Middle Ages. The birth of Christ divided the temporal process: before the event there had been a time of darkness and error; afterwards came the period of light and the triumph of faith. To the Christian, the incarnation of the Son of God was an event written into time; it was God's entry into history to give it its dynamism; it was He who made it the history of salvation.

Nevertheless, God prepared mankind for the coming of His Son through His revelations to the patriarchs and prophets. This concept of universal history as the unfolding of God's plan for His people is present in Holy Scripture itself, but it was made the subject of explicit analysis little by little in the patristic era. St. Augustine of Hippo was the first to expound the theory that just as the world was created in seven days, so there would be seven ages of the world itself. In the last pages of "The City of God", he says:

> Then shall we know this thing perfectly, and we shall perfectly rest and shall perfectly see that He is God. If, therefore, that number of ages be accounted as of days according to the distinctions of time, which seem to be expressed in the sacred scriptures, that Sabbath days shall appear more evidently, because it is found to be the seventh. The first age, as it were the first day, is from Adam unto the flood, and the second from thence unto Abraham, not by equally of times, but by number of generations. For they are found to have the number ten. From hence now, as

Matthew the evangelist doth conclude, three ages do follow even unto the Coming of Christ, every one of which is expressed by fourteen generations. From Abraham unto David is one, from thence unto the incarnate nativity of tChrist. So all of them are made five. Now this age is the sixth, to be measured by no number...After this age God shall rest as on the seventh day...But this shall be our Sabbath, whose end shall not be the evening, but the Lord's day, as the eighth eternal day, which is sanctified and made holy by the resurrection of Christ, prefiguring not only the eternal rest of the spirit, but also the body. (3)

Thus, St. Augustine believes that history is made to reflect the same pattern as the six days of creation and the Sabbath rest that followed. Augustine's last age is, in fact, the age of the departed souls. The eighth age, in these terms, inaugurates eternity. These divisions of history are biblical in origin. (4)

The Venerable Bede gave the "seven ages" idea wide currency in his studies of biblical chronology. He first introduced it in his "Liber de Temporibus", written on 703, in which he briefly sets out the six ages of the world. In his full study, "De temporum rations", written in 725, he adds a seventh and eighth age. Most medieval histories include these divisions in world history. As we shall see later in this work, the "Cursor Mundi" arranges its 25, 000-odd lines upon this structure, but it divides Christ's life into two ages: the fifth age begins with prophecies and the genealogy of Mary, and proceeds through the Childhood of Jesus; the sixth age begins with the Baptism of Christ by St. John the Baptist in the river Jordan. Jechonias and the Transmigration of the Jews to Babylon, that commenced the fifth age in St. Augustine's scheme, are referred to briefly in the closing lines of the fourth age. (5)

In the Middle Ages there also existed a threefold division of human time, that could be superimposed upon the scheme of the seven ages of the world. The "Polychronicon" defines it as the "distinction of tymes": "Oon to fore lawe i-write, þe seconde undit þe lawe i-write, þe seconde undir þe lawe i-write, and þe pride under grace and marcy". (6) The period of natural law lasted from the expulsion of Adam and Eve from Paradise until the Old Law was given to Moses by God on Mount Sinai. During this time, men were in ignorance and only knew darkly God's intentions and His laws. The period of the written law lasted from the time of Moses to the public preaching of Jesus Christ. Christ introduced the law of Charity, and fufulled the old law. The poet of the "Cursor Mundi", as we see today, is living in the time of Grace which will continue until the last trumpet is sounded and doomsday arrives.

This is noted by V.A. Kolve who remarks in "The Play Called Corpus Christi":

> Causality and chronological sequence supply the secular mind with an objective time-order, but for Medieval Christian thought the dignity of past time consists precisely in those trace of future written, by God's shaping of events, upon it. (7)

As a result, the progression from episode to episode in religious histories is often without consecutive impulse. It is not built upon a theory of direct causation: Noah's thank-offering does not cause the offering of Isaac by Abraham, not in any sense lead to it, even though the two actions appear in sequence, with complete disregard of the intervening years. Only the life of Christ has so total a significance that it is dealt with directly in sequential episodes. The rationale behind the time structure of most Medieval religious histories must be described in other terms.

The events chosen for inclusion in sacred histories are those in which God intervenes in human history; significant time, it follows, becomes simply the point of intersection between their actions: the will of God expressed in time from outside time – a causality divine rather than temporal. Erich Auerbach compares the conception of time that is based on a strict sequence of causation, --which he calls horizontal, --to the time implied in a figural relationship between events, which he calls vertical. (8) His distinctions can provide a useful way of thinking about the larger time structure of the history from the same centre, like the casting of a fisherman standing in midstream and making strikes in several degress of a circle. The sequence of these essays has meaning and moves steadily closer to a goal, but the time between them matter very little. The shape of Medieval religious histories (9) is a linear progression, a sequence of self-contained episodes, but the metaphysic of its structure is centrifugal. The relationship between Noah and Abraham exists in God, not in historical events intervening between them. In the same way, St. Augustine's seven ages of the world are primarily vertical in their connection, initiated by acts if God or by new kinds of covenant with Him; the horizontal connections between them are ignored. No age grows by organic development from another but each is abruptly initiated by God, from outside time. Many authors insert brief statements of non-Jewish historical events to emphasize the fact that Christ came to redeem all men. The only portion of world history that is treated consecutively, as we have noted, deals with the life of Christ, the pivotal point. At this time, God the Son does not remain outside of time, but becomes Man.

Further, a distinct kind of anachronism is made possible through this concept of time as artifact. This anachronism permits the poet to refer to Christ in Old Testament contexts, because Our Lord exists both before His incarnation and after His crucifixion; His relationship to time is not horizontal but vertical, due to His triune nature in eternity. God is outside time, and knowledge of His workings can transcend the limitations of any single historical moment.

Medieval man thought of all history as concentrated in a single conflict concerning the fall of man through original sin, and his redemption by the sacrifice of Christ. He had no need of external unity in order to relate all the events of sacred history. His was sure he was living in the time of Mercy; patiently awaiting the Second Coming. The Medieval "present time" was a period of amendment that was regarded as a brief space between the apostolic age and judgment day. This passage from a medieval sermon can usefully illustrate this point:

> And þer-fore arise, for now is tyme for to amend, for now is þe day sterre upe…I undirstond by þe day sterre noþinge els but þis time, þat is now tyme of grace. For had oon man doon all þe synnes þat all þe world might do, ánd he wolde repente him and amend him, he shuld have grace. But aftur þis tyme, when þi bodie is ded, had a man muche repentance as all þe world might have, but he amend him or þat he die, els he shall never have grace withowten ende. (10)

The poet was very conscious of the part providence plays in the affairs of man. As critics have pointed out, in an age of religious faith, it is not surprising that the moment judged to be most important in human history, which centre around Christ's life and death, is never celebrated without reference both ways to the creation anf fall, and to Doomsday, to the first coming and the last. God deals with man as Creator the first time, Saviour the second and will come as Judge on Doomsday. (11) A proper understanding of these three Advents are basic and central for a correct comprehension of the structure of the "Cursor Mundi", and the underlying purpose of its author. There is a logical progression from the first (the Creation of Man) leading to the second (the Redemption of Man) that in turn leads to a last coming.

Thus human time is the artifact of God; it is shaped by Him and expressed His truth, through a multitude of correspondences, congruences, and paradoxes. Time concerns us because we are alive in it and because God's plan for man's redemption can be worked out only in its terms. But man's real business is eternity, and Medieval religious writers never forget to remind him of that. Their aim was to instruct men in the instruments of man's salvation, his passage through time into eternity.

b)   **The Didactic Revival of the 13th Century**

The thirteenth century didactic movement received its primary stimulus from the Fourth Lateran Council of 1215. The century is characterized by a succession of theological, homiletic and liturgical documents designed to educate first the clergy, then the laity in the doctrines of the Church. To provide a clearer view of the "Cursor Mundi"'s position withn the didactic revival, the most important products of this period will be considered under two main divisons: earlier works in Latin intended for the clergy, and later works in the vernacular designed for the laity as well as for churchmen.

Appendix "A"
Figure and Fulfullment

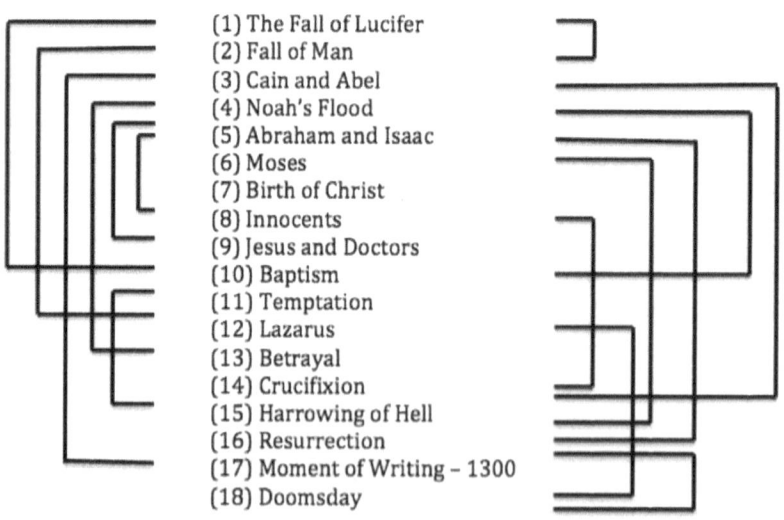

This diagram indicates relationships between various episodes of sacred history that were recognized by Medieval theologians.

The ecumenical council, convened by Pope Innocent III, was the most brilliant gathering of church fathers during the Middle Ages. It marks the culminating point of the pontificate which itself represents the zenith attained by the Medieval papacy. Prelates assembled from every country of Christendom, and with them, the deputies of numerous princes. The total included 412 bishops, and 800 points of discipline were decided, measures were drawn up against heretics, and finally, the regulations for the next Crusade to free Jerusalem from the "infidels" were formulated. One of the important resolutions passed was that free schools for clerics be established in connection with every catherdral. Another canon set down by the assembly required preaching to be undertaken in cathedrals and churches as often as possible by capable men ("viros idoneos").

After the Fourth Lateran Council, the movement to promote spritiual education became an official policy of the Church. Universities and other seats of learning were founded across Western Europe. The two great orders of mendicant-friars were established at this time; the Dominican Order was founded in 1216, and the Franiscan officially recognised in 1220. Spritual education then took on a new aspect because the friars aimed at reaching the laity by means of the art of preaching. This had results in England. In 1240 Walter of Cantelup issued as bshop of Worcestor a set of "Constitutione" in which he proposed that instructional materials such as the manual of confession be made for the facility of parish priests. (12) Archbishop Peckham of Canterbury in 1281 issued a set of "Constitutione" which is even more famous; in these he instigated the systematic teaching of religious knowledge to laymen. So that priests might first improve their own knowledge, Peckham, who was primate of all England from 1279 to 1299, included a summary of the fourteen articles of faith; the ten commandments; the two precepts of the Gospels; the seven works of mercy, the seven deadly sins and cardinal virtues, and the seven Sacraments.

The significant works of the didactic revival can be classified under 1, theological manuals, 2, homiletic matter, and, 3, liturgical matter. Many of them must have been known to the "Cursor" poet, and several were used by him in the composition of his monumental religious poem.

Earlier works in Latin were chiefly intended for the education and instruction of members of the clergy, while later works in the vernacular (French or English) were ensigned for use by the laity as well as by clerics. Although most of the great theological manuals designed for priests are products of the thirteenth century, they represent earlier traditions important toward the development of such works. The most influential manual of a strictly theological nature before the Great Lateran Council was Honoris of Autun's "Elucidarium". He compiled it as a reference book for regular and secular clergy. (13)

The Friars with their great interest in the art of preaching were responsible for producing manuals and collections of sermons for use in their work. It must be noted, however, that their homilies were written in Latin, even though they often preached in the vernacular. Collections of the lives of the saints appear to have developed from Calendars of the feast in the liturgical year. In the course of time, the list of names were expanded in included a few details about the saints themselves. The didactic revival hagiographical collections of the Medieval era. The two most influential collections of the Latin saints' legends are Vincent of Beauvais' "Speculum historicale" and Jacobo de Voragine's "Legenda aurea" respectively. The former work contains succinct lives arranged according to historical dates. The "Legenda aurea" is a true legend arranged according to the liturgical year from Advent to mid-November. The saints' lives are expanded and contain much apocryphal material. Both compilers were Dominicans. Both these collections of saints' legends were used as sources for sermons rather than works intended to be used by laymen. They had considerable influence upon later redactions of vernaculars legends, and works such as the "Cursor Mundi". The "Legenda aurea" is one of the sources of the "South English Legendary", (14) which was written in the midlands a few years prior to the "Cursor Mundi".

The clergy encouraged the translation of Latin works into the vernacular so that they would be more readily understood by the laity. (15) The earliest group of vernacular religious works consists of, for the most part, Old French or Anglo-Norman translations of Latin pieces. One that is used later by the "Cursor" poet, is Robert Grossetestés's "Château d'Amour" (ca. 1225). Grosseteste, a Franciscan bishop of Lincoln, was probably the greatest scholar of his time and he stressed the importance of lay instruction and especially transmission of such information through preaching. (16) This great man, who was on humble origin, said in a Latin preface to "Château d'Amour" that he wrote it in French for those who could not read or understand Latin. (17) At this same time, Honorius' "Elucidarium" was adapted and translated into the Anglo-Norman work entitled "Manuel des peches". (18) This work in turn was adapted into Middle English by Robert Mannyng of Brunne in 1303 as "Handlyng Synne". Mannyng directs it principally toward the laity, not the clergy. He states at least three times that the work is for the unlearned layman, or "lewde" man because a priest should already know what he has to say. (19) To this end he renders the original into more simple language and the tone of "Handlying Synne" is quite colloquial. From the beginning of the fourteenth century there commences a series of theological manuals in English, written largely for the benefit of laymen rather than for church men. The "Cursor Mundi" is written in this tradition. The poet asks the question:

> Frenkis rimes here i rede
> Comunli in ilka stede;
> Þat es most made for frankis men,
> Quat helpis him Þat non can cen.

"Seldom", he adds, "is the English tongue praised in France; he will give to each nation their own language and there is no outrage in doing so." The increasing use of the vernacular was one of the results, as we have noted, of the Fourth Lateran Council.

Although the immediate impetus for writing works on religious topics was the didactic movement of the thirteenth century, and the emphasis placed upon the art of preaching by the friars, an earlier tradition, especially in England, mus not be forgotten. The traditons of homiletic writing in the vernacular was well established in the tenth century. The sermons of Aelfric and Wulfstan that have survived testify to the importance of homilies in English. The tradition of hagiographical cycles of English homilies on the "santorale" and "temporale" go back to the "Blickling Homilies" also of the tenth century. (21) An essential difference, however, must be noted between the earlier homilies and those that appeared in the thirteenth century. The former belong to a monastic tradition of sermons that are learned and stabilized, while the latter, the more popular, are created under mendicant influence, aiming to entertain as well as inform.

Not all of the English sermons of the Norman period have survived, but we know of them by references in other work which gives continuity to English literature during the so-called fallow centuries. (22) For example, Jocelyn of Brakelord gives a description of a vernacular delivery of a homily in his "Chronica" (ca. 1202). Abbot Samson, he says, had a pulpit built in the abbey church of Saint Edmund, "ad utilitatem audientium et ad decorum ecclesiae"; from this "useful" and "decorative" pulpit the abbot often used to read Scripture and his sermons in English, even though, comments the Chronicler, he was fluent in both French and Latin. (23)

One of the most ambitious collections of sermons in Middle English that was undertaken at this time was by an Augustinean Canon, named Orm, in the Midlands. Orm proposes in his preface to his "little book", "Ormulum" (24) (ca. 1200) to compose or translate 242 sermons. Although thirty-two are extant, the work comprises almost twenty thousand short lines. The author directs his work chiefly towards his fellow clerics, that they may "spellen to Þe folle/Off Þe ezzre sawle nede." For the need of souls Orm proposed to render a verse translation of all the Gospels contained in the Missal and to include an exegesis on each. It is possible that Orm's spelling was a kind of phonetic index for pulpit reading. (25) In any case his good intentions do seem to have been utilized much for vernacular presentation: the work exists in only one manuscript, probably the author's own.

Extant in early Middle English are several anonymous and isolated sermons. The alliterative prose "Sawles Warde" dates from the beginning of the thirteenth century and is contained in the Katherine Group. The greatest number of English sermons, however, occur in collections or groups. A few collections date from the twelfth century and suggest some continuity with monastic Anglo-Saxon homilies of the tenth century, particularly those by Aelfric and Wulfstan, although more recent Latin and Anglo-Norman influence are evident.

In Old French or Anglo-Norman homiletic material in England strikes a differnet tone than what remains in English. The fact that Robert of Greatham's "Miroir", or as it is often called, "Les Evangiles of Domees" was in Anglo-Norman and composed for the Lady Eleanor de Montfort and her court illustrates an essential difference between French and English devotional literature of this period. (26) French works were usually destined for a sophisticated and educated audience, either lay or clerical; English works usually appealed to a more limited clergy or laity. When the "Miroir" was later adapted into English as part of the "North English Homily Collection", the anonymous translator added a prologue saying that his work was intended for the unlettered who come to the parish church on Sunday to say their prayers and receive instruction. (27)

If the approach differed, however, the authors' purpose and general techniques were similar. Greatham translated the Gospels into French because, as he says, it was a "mult grant folie" to speak Latin to laymen who could not profit from it. As Eleanor's chaplain he hoped to lure her away from the "chansons de geste" and chronicles he laments she is so fond of hearing. To attract interest to something more edifying he resorts to a jingling rhythm and remarkable feats of rhyme. The same complaints against the popular vogue for romances are found in the "Prologue" of the "Cursor Mundi", which will be examined in the next chapter. The "Cursor" poet, who addresses his audiences as "lewd", like Greatham, attempts to draw his listeners away from the world of men with a sweep of biblical matter in the most popular of homiletic styles.

A tread towards the increasing use of the vernacular is clearly seen throughout the thirteenth century in both theological and homiletic material. This trend is even more pronounced in that area of liturgical writing dealing with hagiography. (28) The number of vernacular saints' legends, isolated or in collections, in verse or prose, reaches its greatest height in the thirteenth and fourteenth centuries. The trend within this "genre" is not surprising. Saints' legends had always exhibited a tendency toward popularization. The church authorities, at times, had attempted to curb the spreading of certain legends. In the twelfth century, John Beleth, the author of the often-printed "Rationale divinorum officiorum", had tried to ban the legend of the Saints Gregory, Quiriacus, and Julita from inclusion in passionaries' and legendaries. (29) Yet, these apocryphal legends continued to circulate, first in Latin and then in the vernacular; Quiriacus' legend is referred to in the "Cursor Mundi". (30) The danger involved in vernacular translation even of the more orthodox legends had very early been recognized. When Aelfric of Winchester translated his collection of "Passiones martyrum" into Old English prise in 995, he gave as his reason a desire to stimulate a failing faith by means of the martyrs' example. It would only be possible, he believed, in a language the faithful could understand. (31)

During the twelfth and thirteenth centuries vernacular saints' legends began to replace homilies in Latin read on the appropriate feast days. Extant in collections or singly these hagiographical legends represent an impressive body of medieval vernacular literature. A large number of single, isolated legends in verse represent a high degree of craftsmanship and suggest composition for special occasions and sophisticated audiences. An anonymous Anglo-Norman verse life of Edward the Confessor, for example, describes to the listening "seignurs" such an event within the poem itself. On a certain day, says the author, high Mass was sung in honour of Edward before the nobleman who had come from the city to pay homage to the saint on his feast day. The author describes how, after the Gospels was read, a sermon was given on the subject of the saintly king and his great worthiness. Although the device is a narrative commonplace (cf. the recitation of lays in "Beowulf", for example), this particular description is suggestive of how and when legends were read, a question of some importance in understanding the "Cursor Mundi".

By way of summary, then, a tradition of lay instruction had been established in England by the middle of the thirteenth century. Not all of it was the product of the didactic movement after 1215, since a few religious works in Latin and the vernacular had been in circulation sometime before then. By mid-thirteenth century lay education existed on two levels. The largest number of works sought to educate priests directly by means of theological manuals, liturgical collections, or sermons – usually in Latin. A smaller number sought to educate the layman himself in his own vernacular. The friars played an important role on both levels, but they were by no means responsible for the didactic works of the period, nor were they the authors of the most popular, secularized examples.

The "Cursor Mundi", therefore, has a wealthy tradition of religious literature behind it. The tradition is rich in both languages (Latin and two vernaculars) and form (sermons and legends). Of all representatives of this large body of religious writing, this poem is one of the most ambitious in scope and successful in execution. The "Cursor Mundi", as we shall see, has a unity that the "South English Legendary" (32) (ca. 1275) and the "Northern Homily" cycle (33) (ca. 1300) lack.

By placing this religious poem in the historical context, we can see more plainly that it is the culmination of a long tradition of didactic works for the instruction of the faithful. Other writers before the "Cursor" poet had determined a hierarchy of significant events in Scripture, and their choice decisively influenced all art forms during the fourteenth century. A number of known and anonymous writers were engaged in translating and making clearer for the "lewde" people a story whose shape and meaning and already been definitely formulated by the Doctors of the Church. (34) The basic source for the "Cursor Mundi" was, of course, the Bible, but patristic commentary determined the form the matter would take. By judicious use of popular religious commentary and by occasional direct reference to the Fathers, the poet had access to a body of critical thought that was instrumental in the making of the poem. The selection of the most fruitful matter from the Scriptures had been made long before the "Cursor Mundi" had been written. As the nature of his undertaking required, the poet derived material from various sources. Besides the Vulgate, he used Peter Comestor's Latin "Historicia Scolastica", (35) Herman of Valenciennes' "Bible", (36) Wace's "L'Establissement de la Fête de la Conception Notre Dame", (37) Robert Grossesteste's "Château d'Amour", (38) the "Pseudo-Matthaei Evangelicum", (39) the "Southern Assumption", (41) Isodore's "De Vita et Morte Sanctorum", (42) the "Legenda aurea" (43) and other works. The poet simply took over certain significant patterns that had previously been observed and studied in the Bible narrative, and by simplifying, abridging, or neglecting entirely the mass of incident and detail that surround them, produced a unified sequence charged with meaning which was strong, simple and yet formally coherent. (44)

Within this background, the "Cursor Mundi" enclosed in the Medieval acceptance of Our Lady as the Mediatrix of the graces of Our Lady as the Mediatrix of the graces of the Redemption, for this poem, the poet has told us, is written in her honour. Christ is looked upon as a stern judge; Mary is regarded as the smiling mother who pleads for us. This is noted by Graef:

> Mary was now becomg more "human", so to speak, she was seen as a woman sharing all the joys and the sufferings of women. If God, even the incarnate God, her Son, was still felt to be in some way remote from men, because He was a divine Person, Mary was wholly a mother, smiling at her child, weeping over Him when he had died. True, she was now enthroned in heaven also primarily as a mother, placed there to help her children struggling on earth. (45)

The "Cursor" poet confidently declares his faith in the Virgin Mary:

> Scho prais ay for sinful men.   108
> Qua þat worschipis hir he mai be bald,
> Scho wil him ȝeilde an hundredth fald, (46)

As we shall see, he rounds out his long poem returning to Our Lady after his description of the Last Judgement:

> And syden of þe dome sal i say,   216
> Þan of vr leudis murnand mode
> For hir sune quen he hing on rode;
> Þe last resune of all þis roune
> Sal be of hir concepcion. (47)   220

He ends his work with a charming legend about Our Lady. The poet always gives honour to the Virgin Mary. He presents her in a manner that would appeal to his audience and his readers. The Middle Ages loved Our Lady next only to Christ. And in narrating His life, Medieval man allowed her story its proper dignity within it.

Chapter II
Purpose of the Poem

The "Cursor Mundi" is, literally, the "courser" of the world from its creation to the Last Judgement. In the two hundred and seventy line Prologue, the anonymous poet clearly states his aims in writing this monumental work. Unlike the author of the "Ormulum" or the creator of "The Canterbury Tales", the "Cursor" poet, even though his project was vast, embracing all the most significant events of Christian history, completed his plan. He realized it not unworthily. He was familiar with most of the secular poetry popular across Western Europe at the close of thirteenth century. He had read the French romances, their English imitations, and often frivolous songs of clerics writing in Latin, but he could devlop no enduring taste for this literature. He opens his poem with a rousling description of the romances that the medieval inhabitants of Britian enjoyed reading or listening to:

[Me]u ȝernis iestis for to here,
And romance rede on maner ser,
Of alexander þe conquerour,   4
Of Iuli cesar þe cmperour
[Of grece & Tr]oye þe strong strijf,
[Þere many thosand lesis] hir lijf,
[O brut Þ]at berne bolde of hand
[First Conqu]erour of meri ingland;   8
[Of] king arthour, þat was so riche,

> [W[as non in his time funden suiche;
> Of ferlijs þat his knigh[t]es fell,
> [Of] auntris did i here of tell,   12
> [Of] wawain, kay, and other stabil,
> [For] to were þe runde tabil.
> Hou king charlis and rouland fight—
> Wid sarazins ne wald þai neuer be sight;--   16
> Þat foly loue þat vanite.
> ham likes now na 'oþer gle.
> hit ys bot fantum soþ to say
> to day hit ys to morne a-way.   20
> Þorow chaunce of dede or ellis of hert
> Þat soft bigan has endyng smert.
> Sangys sere of diuers rime,
> Engliss, franss, and latine,   24
> To rede and here, ilkon is prest,
> Of thinges þat þaim liked best.
> Þe wisman wil of wisdam here,
> Þe fole him drauis to foli nere,   28
> Þe wrong to here right es loth,
> And pride wid buxumnes es wroght;
> Of chastite has lecchour lite;
> Charite again wreth wil smete;   32
> Bot bi þe f[r]uyt may ilk man se
> Of quat uertu es ilk a tre.
> Þis fruit bitakins all oure dedis
> Bath gode and ill qua right redis;   36
> vr dedes fra vr hert tas rote
> Queþer þai turne to bale or bote, (1)

In this stirrling opening passage of the "Cursor Mundi", we have a listing of the various types of romances that men yearned to hear in the Middle Ages. These romances which were at the height of their vogue at this time, come from the three Matters. (2) There were cycles of stories about Alexander the Great, the Seige of Troy, King

Arthur and his Knights of the Round Table, and Charlemagne and his paladins, which are mentioned by the "Cursor" poet. He also refers to such well-known single romances as Tristan and Isolde, (3) Sir Isumbras, and Amadas and Idoine. (4) The poet notes that each man likes to read of the things nearest his heart, (5) be they of princesm prelates or of kings, written in varying rimes in Latin or the vernacular tongues of French or English.

The "Cursor" poet goes on to observe that the wise man delights to hear of wisdom, while the fool lends his ear to folly. He questions the value of reading or hearing tales of strange and wonderful happenings. The condemning of popular romances by churchmen was not uncommon during the Middle Ages. Robert of Greatham, who was quoted in the last chapter, is a good example.

At this point, the poet gives a small sermon on the evils of the present age which only esteem those who have paramours, saying men are known for good or ill by what they are attracted to:

For be Þat thing men draus till	
Men may Þaim knaue for gode and ill,	
A sample hereby til Þaim i say	
Þat ragis in to Þair riot alway,	48
In riot and in rekelage	
Of all Þair lijf spend Þai Þer stage;	
For nu es holdyn non in cours	
Bot he Þat can loue paramours; --	52
Þat foli l[u]ue Þat vanyte	
Him likes nou non oÞer gle.	
It es bot fanton for to say	
To day it es, to moru away,	56
Wid chance of dede or change of hert	
Þat soft bigan endis ful smert.	
For quen Þu wenis traistiest to be,	
Þu sal fra hir or scho fra Þe,	60
He Þat wenis stiffest to stand,	
War him hijs fal is neist at hand. (6)	

He notes that earthly things as earthly love is here today, gone tomorrow. He dwells on the transitory nature of earthly things and that man appears strongest when his fall is close at hand. The poet, after reminding us that all is unsure in this world, tells us to have devotion to the Virgin Mary who is Man's best friend and always remains true. This is how he describes Our Lady:

> ForÞi i blise Þat paramoure
> Þat in mi [nede me dos socure],
> Þat sauis me in erde fra sinne,
> And heuen bliss me helpis to winne,   72
> For Þou i sumtime be untrewe
> Hir luue es euerelike neue;
> Hir luue scho haldes treu and lele,
> Ful suete it es to manes hele,
> Suilk in erd es funden non
> For scho es moÞer and maiden alon,
> MoÞer and mayden neuer Þe less,
> For Þi of hir toke iesu his fless. (7)   80

He goes on to say that men who can compose poems or write stories should do so in honour and praise of Our Lady and her Son:

> Wat bot es to set trauail
> On thing Þat noght may auail,
> Þat es bot fantom of Þis werld
> As ȝe haue sene i-now and herd.(8)   92

He points out that we know enough of her fairness and her love to make many poems about Our Lady:

> Qua will of hir fayrness spell
> Find he may inogh to tell;   96
> Of hir godnes of hit trouth-hedd,
> Men may find euermar to rede

>   Of reuth of luue and of charite;
>   Was neuer hir make ne neuer sal be. (9)   100

The "Cursor" poet then announces that he will undertake such a lasting work in honour of the Blessed Virgin Mary, which will be founded on the wonderfully steadfast ground that is the Holy Trinity, because:

>   Scho prais ay for sinful men.   108
>   Qua þat worschipis hir he mai be bald,
>   Scho wil him ȝeilde an hundredth fald,
>   [I]N hir worschip wald i biginne
>   A lastand werk apon to mine.   112
>   For to do men knaue hir kin
>   Þat us suilk worschip gan to win,
>   Sumkin ieste nu forto knau
>   Þat don was in þe alde lau;   116
>   Bituix þe ald lau and þe new
>   Hu cristes bote bigan to brew,
>   I sal ȝou scheu wid min entent,
>   Sothli of hir testament.   120
>   All þis werld, ar þis boke bline,
>   Wid cristes help i sal our-rine,
>   And telle sun ieste principale.
>   For all may no man haue in tale,   124
>   Bot forþer may na werk stand
>   Widvten grund-wal to be lasand,
>   Þarfor þis werke i wil found
>   On a seleuth stedfast grund,   128
>   Þat es þe hali trinite,
>   Þat all has made wid his bounte. (10)

Thus against the vanity and folly of the world, the poet had put the seriousness of the Christian way of life; against sensual love, the adoration of God and the worship of the Virgin Mary.

He states that in honour of the Mother of God, he will write a poem which should teach of the decree of God, as embodied in her, its causes as well as its results, and will show from the beginning of history of the race from which Mary sprang. Furthermore he will write in English so that his work will have as wide a reading public as possible.

The "Cursor" poet then proceeds to give a brief summary of the topics that he proposes to deal with in his work. The "Cursor Mundi", in fact, contains most of the significant passages of sacred history besides a great deal of legendary material. Beginning with the Trinity, on which the work is to rest as on a firm foundation, the poet sets himself to describe the creation of the world, the fall of the angels, the fall of Ada, and the fortunes of his immediate posterity;

>   First at himself i sett mi marke,
>   And siÞen to tell of his handwarke, --   132
>   Of Þe angelis first Þat fell,
>   And siÞen i wil of adam tell,
>   Of his hospring (11)

Next he proceeds to indicate which events in the Old Testament he plans to include in his long poem.

>   and of noe,
>   And sunquat of his sunes thre.   136
>   Of abraham and of ysaac,
>   Þat hali mẹn war widuten lac;
>   SiÞen sal i tell to ȝou
>   Of iacob and of ysau,   140
>   Here neist sal be siÞen teld
>   Hu Ioseph was bath bogh[t] and seld
>   Of Þe iuus and of moyses
>   Þat goddess folk to lede him ches;   144
>   Hou godd bigan Þe lai him giue,

> Þe quilk Þe iuus suld in liue.
> Of saul Þe king and of daui
> How Þat he faught again goli, 148
> And syðe of salamon Þe wise
> Hou crafttili he did iustiifie. (12)

The poet then say that he will narrate how Christ came as the fulfillment of the prophecies, after which he intends to deal with the story of Joachim and Saint Anne and the birth of Mary and how she gave birth to Christ, when and where, and of the events of His childhood:

> How crst cam thoru prophesy
> His aune folk forto bi; 152
> SiÞen it sal be rede 3ou Þano
> Of ioachim and of saint ane;
> Of mari als hir douther milde
> Hou scho him to Þe temple bare; 156
> Of Þe kinges Þat him soght
> Þat thre presantes til him broght;
> Hou Þat iesu til egipt fled
> And hu Þat he was Þennis ledd. 160
> And Þer suld 3e here mani a dede
> Þat iesu did in his barnhede; (13)

Next the poet says he will tell of Christ's baptism, one of the beheading of John the Baptist and some of the most important incidents in Our Lord's public life:

> SiÞen of Baptist saint iohn,
> Þat iesu Baptist in Þe flom iordan. 168
> Hou iesu wan he longe hade fast
> Wastemped wid Þe wicked gast;
> SiÞen of ionis baptizing
> And hou him hefded heroud king. 172

> Hu Þai iesu crist him seluen
> Ches to him apostilis tuelue,
> And opinli bigain to preche,
> And all Þat seke war to leche,   176
> And did miraclis sua rif,
> Quarfor Þe iuus him held in strijf;
> SiÞen hu god all-mightin
> Turnd water into win;   180
> Of fijf thousand men Þat he
> Fedd wid fijf louis and fisses thre;
> Of a man sal ȝe siÞen find
> Þat god gaf sight Þat born was blind,   184
> And of Þe spousebreche, Þat woman
> Þat Þe iuus demed to stan;
> How he heled a man vnfere
> Þat seke was eght and tuenti ȝere;   188
> Hou mari magdalain wid grete
> Com to wasse vr lauerdes fete,
> Of hir and Martha Þat wild noght blin
> Aboute Þe nedis of hir inne,   192
> Of lazar Þat ded lay vnder stan,
> Hou iesu him raysd in fless and ban; (14)

The "Cursor" poet informs us that he will describe Christ's passion, death, descent into hell, and resurrection:

> Hou Þai sched his blissed blode,
> And pined him apon Þe rode.
> Wid cristes will Þan sal i tell
> Hou he siÞen harud hell,   200
> Hu iuus wid Þair grete vnskill
> Wend his vprising to dill; (15)

This section, which includes the Crucifixion and the Harrowing of Hell, is the climax of the "Cursor Mundi". After dealing with the descent of the Holy Ghost, the poet tells us that he intends to treat Our Lady's end and the finding of the holy cross before proceeding to narrate the events at the end of the world:

> Of antecrist come Þat sal be kene,
> And of Þe dreri dais fijftene
> Þat sal cum bifor domesday; (16)

But before he lays aside his pen, confirming the purpose of this poem, the author declares that he will return to Mary by describing her agony at the foot of the cross before ending the work with a contemporary miracle of Our Lady. This final incident tells how an eleventh century abbot of Ramsey was saved from shipwreck by promising to establish a feast in honour of Mary's miraculous conception:

> Þe last resune of all Þis roune
> Sal be of hir concepcion. (17)   220

This return to Pur Lady at the close of this very long poem tends to gives a balance to the poem. The "Cursor" poet truly frames his monumental religious saga in the contemporary devotion to the Mother of Our Saviour,

The "Cursor" poet is convinced that many incidents in the religious history of the world are as exciting and marvelous as any to be found in the popular contemporary romances. In writing this work, he is motivated by a desire to give praise to Our Lady, to popularize some of the most important events in sacred history, and to produce a poem that could readily be understood by his English-speaking countrymen. He declares:

> Nedeful me think it were to man
> To knau him self, hou he bigan.
> Hou he bigan in world to brede,
> Hou his ospring bigan to sprede,   228

> Bath of Þe first and of Þe last,
> In quatkin cours Þis werld is past. (18)

The poet finishes his "Prologue" with his remarks on why he has written it in English, which we have referred to above in the introduction. His poem is especially written to help those who cannot read or understand French. He notes in conclusion that:

> Coursur of Þe werld men au it call,
> For all mast it ouer-rines all.   268
> Take we vr biginyng Þan
> Of him Þat all Þis werld bigan. (19)

Although not unique in plan in European letters, it was so in English:

> There is no lack of compositions in the Ages following a plan similar to that of the "Cursor Mundi". Nothing of the kind existed in the English language, however. The most attractive legends and traditions that occupied the age were now first blended for the English people, with the most momentous passages of Bible history. It formed a great fabric in which earlier and later things were interwoven, as promise and fulfilment, picture and reality. The plan of the whole is similar to that of the "Collective Mysteries", that now began to take form, not uninfluenced by the "Cursor Mundi". (20)

The merit of the poet is so much greater as he was not in a position to base his poem on any single text, as did the authors of the Genesis and Exodus, nor did he desire to do so. He collected his material from several writings, though perhaps not from so many as we might assume in our inadequate knowledge of the sources accessible to him. Aside from Holy Writ, the material was taken, as we shall see in the following chapters, from biblical exegists and homilists; further, many apocryphal books were used, some of them, perhaps, at second-hand. The "Cursor" poet's remarkable skill is to be found in the way he blended the numerous sources into a unified account of Man's fall and redemption.

The poet's purpose in writing the "Cursor Mundi" is not unlike Robert Grosseteste's stated aims when he wrote "Château d'Amour" early in the thirteenth century. In fact, the "Cursor" poet includes a free translation of Grosseteste's French work, which is a kind of religious romance, dealing with the fundamental articles of Christian belief under the guise of chivalry, a pious "Roman de la Rose". The famous bishop of Lincoln, who was the first chancellor of the University of Oxford, offers his "religious" romance dealing with the four daughters of God and the Castle of Love, which is Our Lady, without an apology. Unlike the "Cursor" poet, there is no comparison with worldly romances. Grosseteste's prologue opens merely with expressions of piety:

> Ki bien pense bien poet dire;
> Sanz penser ne poez suffire
> De nul bien fet commencer;
> Deus nus doint de li penser,
> De ki, par ki, en ki sunt
> Tuz les biens ki sunt el mund. (21)

He wrote this work for the laity, and expounded a difficult subject in terms familiar to his audience, to be used for the benefit of the clergy. He puts his purpose thus:

> Tuz avum mestier de aïe,
> Mes trestuz ne poüm mie
> Saver le langage en fin
> D'ebreu, de griu ne de latin,
> Pur loer sun creatur.
> Ke la buche de chantëur

Ne seit close de Deu loer
Ne sun seint nun nuncier
E ke chescun en sun langage
En li conuisse sanz folage,
Son Deu e sa redempcion,
En romanz comenz ma reson
Pur ceus ki ne sevent mie
Ne lettrëure ne clergie. (22)

The "Cursor" poet, like Grossetesté, kept his audience in mind while writing his long poem. His audience would include ordinary people, more familiar with the ways of rural life than civil or commercial affairs. The poet has the greatest respect for authority, explaining several times the importance of tithes. He does not include such descriptions of courtly splendour as we find in the first part of "Sir Gawain and the Green Knight". (23) What he does know of courtly life appears to have come from books. Of course, he may have taken into account the limited background and restricted interests of his audience and readers. He does enjoy including information on practical matters such as the four humours, the effects of old age, the movement of the sun and the moon, and the importance of different kinds of fruit trees. He also likes an exciting story, the marvelous and strange, and appears to enjoy describing the final illness of King Herod in all its horror. (24) He makes things concrete and easily understood by over-simplification. In short, the "Cursor Mundi" represents a microcosm of its audience's range of interest and experience.

As a didactic work, the first object of the poem would be to present the teaching of the church. Yet, its treatment of theological questions represents a very different approach to presentation than do the manuals of instruction. We find no complex theological discussions which are found in some Medieval works such as certain of the plays in the Hegge cycle. (25) The theology in the "Cursor Mundi" is simple, orthodox and applied.

The poet shows great skill in concealing the didactic purpose of his work. He is both "dulce" and "utile". The entertaining narrative and lively style masks the more serious aim, that of teaching the Faith, the nature of God, and His created Universe, the revolt of Lucifer, the Fall of Man and God's plan of redemption all occur within the cyclical framework of the "Cursor Mundi". Nothing heretical or theologically unsound creeps into the work. (26) The poet intended his readers and hearers to respond to the "Cursor Mundi" with heart and devotion.

  With particular skill the poet does achieve his purpose: the long narrative is rendered tight and continuous by interweaving it, as we shall see, with a tight warp of prophecy, myth and legend.

Medival Concept of History
Old Testament

The Sacred Histories	The Two Times	The Three Laws	The Seven Ages of the World	Cursor Mundi	Line (ff)
Old Testament	The Time of Misdoing (Justice)	Natural Law	First	Creation	271
				Adam's Fall	754
				Cain & Abel	1045
				Quest of Seth	1227
			Second	The Flood Noah's Sons	1627
				The Flood Noah's Sons	2081
			Third	Abraham	2315
				Isaac	3117
				Jacob	3411
				Joseph	4037
		Written Law	Fourth	Moses	5495
				Saul	7287
				David of the Wands	7973
			Fifth	Solomn of the Holy Rood	8435

Time as arti act: some medieval divisions of history that would have been well-known to the Cursor poet.

Medieval Concept of History
New Testament

The Sacred Histories	The Two Times	The Three Laws	The Seven Ages of the World	Cursor Mundi	Line (ff)
New Testament Apocryphal Gospels	The Time of Grace (Mercy)	The Law of Charity	Sixth	Baptism of Christ	12,751
				Christ's Ministry	13,242
				Passion	14,937
				Crucifixion	16,665
				Harrowing of Hell	17,848
				Acts of the Apostles	18,863
				Assumption of Mary	20,011
				Apostolic Times	20,849
				Finding of the Cross	21,247
				(Abbot of Ramsy's Vision in 1070 AD)	
				(Moment of Writing – 1300 AD)	
			Seventh (Doomsday)	Day of Doom	21,847
				Antichrist	21.975
				Fifteen Signs of Doom	22,427
				Description of Hell and Heaven	23,195

Chapter III
Use of Prophecy as a Unifying Force

When the "Cursor" poet deals with prefiguring and prophecy, he follows the well-established formula laid down by the early Fathers of the Church. He was not an innovator in this regard. He used prophecy, as he used myth and legend, to strengthen the narrative unity of his long poem.

The poet skillfully connects the various sections of his narrative and he gives explanations of difficult scriptural passages. For example, the poet interprets what God meant when before the flood he said, "I rue that I made man":

> "Me rewis þat euer i made man."
> Bot ilk a man þat þis word heris,
> wat noght all quat it to peris,   1604
> Þis word was as a prophessye,
> Þat for said was bi his merci,
> Of þe reuthe him siþen kidd,
> Quen he to pine him seluen did   1608
> For his schoslinges apon rode tre,
> Quat was his reuthe nu all mau se. (1)

He uses many of the well-known prophecies within his work in an appropriate way. He announces that he will come, through the prophecies, to Christ:

> Bot lauerdinges for-þi þat i
> Thoru witnessing of prophesy,
> And thoru prof of þe seluen dede,
> To birth i wild vr lauerd lede, (2) 6866

Prophecy is found, of course, throughout the Old Testament. Christ quoted many of the prophecies Himself. (3) The early Christians expounded these prophecies. The early Fathers of the Church saw in the patriarchs, such as Abraham, Isaac and Jacob, various prefigurings of Christ. (4) Even the Psalms are carefully explained as prophecies of Christ's birth, life, passion, death, burial, and resurrection. Medieval man was very conscious of the reality of prophecy, and for him the past, the presents and the future were very closely knit together; everything that surrounded him was in some manner an index pointing towards God, towards salvation, or towards damnation. Prophecy is constantly used in the "Cursor Mundi", and in the sources it draws upon, not merely because it provs Christ to be promised and long awaited Messiah, but because it foretells the whole course of human history in order that we may understand that nothing of crucial importance happens by caprice or accident. In the medieval cycles, some of the most powerful pageants are those dealing with prophecies. (5)

In the "Cursor Mundi", the sense of prophecy has been even more skillfully refined. The poet persistently calls to our attention the significance of an action in somewhat the same manner as the Expositer of the Chester Cycle.

The "Cursor" poet quotes some of the famous prophecies of Isaiah as an introduction to the Fifth Age of the World, which deal with the genealogy of Mary, her birth and childhood, before proceeding to the birth and childhood of Jesus. He says:

> Crist was forsaid wid prophesy,
> Þat mast of spac saint ysay,
> And to þe iuus so mistrouand,
> He bad þaim here and vnderstand. (6) 9268

The poet even explains in English the meaning of one prophecy:

> "Gode men," he said, "can ȝe noght se?
> For of a man þat hiht Iesse
> A mayden sal brede, of his hup-spring,
> And scho sal haue a sone to king, 9284
> I wil noght hele for drede of blame,
> Emanuel sal be his name." (7)

The poet adds:

> þat es to say, in englis þus, (9287)
> vr lauerd him-seluen alle wid vs. (8) 9288

"Cursor" poet includes such well-known prophecies of Isaiah about the root of Jesse:

> "Iesse," he said, "of his rotyng
> Certaynly a wand suld spring,
> vte of þat a flour suld brest,
> þe hali gast þar-on suld rest, 9722
> þe gast þat giues giftes sere." (9)

He then quotes Isaiah again concerning the promised Messiah:

> A mayden sal vs bere a childe, 9308
> Querof i tald ȝou here biforn,
> Tille vre bi-houe sal he be born.
> þis child sal vs be gyuen tille,
> And sal reyne at his willel 9312
> Men sal him call wid names sere,
> 'Ferlyful' and 'cunsaylere.'
> Godd of strength and fader es he,
> Cald of þat world es forto be, 9316

And 'prins of pais,' men sal him call,
And neuer mare sal his reyne fall. (10)

The poet also includes Jeremiah's foretelling of the coming of the Savior, and that when Christ comes the Jews will no longer have an anointed King. This is how he handles this prophecy:

>   Quen he þat haliest es comen,
>   3our noynting sal fra 3ou be nomen.
>   Bot 3it i hope 3e be sua blind,
>   Þat 3e can noght mi resun findl   9340
>   King wer 3e wont to noint ay-quare,
>   Bot sua sul 3e nou haue na mare,
>   Fra he ne noynted, þat i say,
>   Kingles sul 3e be fra þat day." (11)   9344

The prophets Joel and Elias are cited in support of Jeremiahs's prophecy. But the Jews took no heed and were faithless:

>   Bot for na talking þaim was tald,
>   It tok neuer in þair hertis hald,
>   Bot ay mistrouing and mistrows. (12)

Many of the prophecies that are selected for inclusion in this poem deal with the Virgin Mary. This is in keeping with the framework that centres on the contemporary devotion to Our Lady. The poet declares that God said the following of Mary:

>   He said, "my lemman es sua gent,
>   Scho smellis suetfer þan piment,   9356
>   And wele softer hir vestiment
>   Þan any reclis þat er brent.
>   Fayr es þe muth of þat leudy,
>   And ilk toth es as yuory,   9360
>   As douues eye hir loke es suete,

As rose on thorn er to vnmete;
And tuene þaim fayre acord es nane,
Sua es tuix hir kin and my lenman." (13)   9364

There is a long section on the events leading up to the birth of the Virgin Mary in the "Cursor Mundi". (14) The thanksgiving offerings of Joachim when he is told by an angel that his wife Anna will have a child is given prophetic significance by the poet. The joyful father-to-be offered ten white lambs, twelve bulls, and one hundred sheep: the lambs to God, the bulls to the poor, and the sheep to the town. This is the significance that the "Cursor" poet gives to Joachim's offerings:

Þe lambis ten all als an
Bitakins iesu crist was tan,   10392
And don on rode for vr wite,
And for vs suffrid gret despite.
Þe bolys tuelue he offrid sua,
Vnderstand tuelue apostlis þa,   10396
Þat tholid for crist soru and care,
And martird for his loue þai ware.
Þis hundred þat war boune,
Were all delt to þe commune,   10400
Bitakins felauschip, i-wiss,
Of saintes hye in heuen bliss,
Þe takning of an hundred tale,
All fullines it takins hale. (15)   10404

    The last straight prophecy that we will cite from this poem is that of Simeon who cried out with joy when he beheld the infant Jesus. The aged Simeon, whose sons take a prominent part in the Harrowing of Hell as we shall see in Chapter VI, foretells Christ will be the downfall of the wicked and the salvation of the good:

"Þis child," he said bi-for þaim alle,

> "Sal be to fele in uprising,
> In takning alsua of gainsaying;   11364
> Þis dunefal sal we vnderstand
> Suld be all Þe mistrouand,
> Þis vprising of oÞerfele
> Þat in trouth w[ar] treu and lele."   11368
> Til mari he said, "Þin auen hert
> A sorful word sal stic ouer-thuert;"
> Þe suord of soru thoru hir hert stod,
> Quan scho hir sune sau hang on rod. (16)   11372

Now, let us turn to another part of prophecy, in which events in the Old Testament are made to pre-figure events of Christ's life. Selection of episodes from the Scriptures for use in the "Cursor Mundi" is often based upon their significance as pre-figuring episodes connected with the Second Advent – the redemption of man by Jesus Christ. These episodes stand for events greater than themselves. This view of the Old Testament is made clear by the fifteenth century bishop of St. Asap and Chichester, Reginald Pecock, who is his "Ruele of Chrysten Religioun" (17) explains that God revealed His coming in the flesh in three ways: by direct announcement to the Fathers, as when he told Abraham that the Messiah would be born by his seed, by announcements through the prophets to the chosen people at large; and by—

> Figuris and tokens afore rennying, booÞ afore Þe lawe youun to Moyses and in the lawe youun to Moyses, and Þat by alle Þe sacrificis and oÞere observanncis youun in Þe lawe of Jewis. (18)

It is frequently this third form of announcement that is selected by the "Cursor" poet from the Old Testament material, to assist in binding and unifying the whole poem. Erich Auerbach gives a good description of "figura":

> It is something real and historical which announces something else that is also real and historical. The relation between the two events is revealed by an accord of similarity. (19)

With this statement to guide is, we may also explore the richer formulation made by St. Basil in the fourth century:

> The types is a manifestation of things to come through an imitation allowing us to see in advance the things of the future in such a ways that they can be understood. (20)

Originally, this interest in the concordance of events arose from the need to prove the unity of the Old and the New Testaments. This technique was used in the defeat of the Gnostic heresy, which held that Christ superseded the "demiurge" of the Jewish Old Testament, as it had been used against the Jews to prove that Christ was indeed their long-promised Messiah. It offered simultaneously an explanation of the Bible as a dual revelation, and a demonstration of the Bible's truth. (21) Figuration produced works during the Middle Ages which tell the story of Christ's birth but pauses at each major incident in the story to explain the relevant Old Testament's episodes thet pre-figure it. Christ Himself used this technique in His teaching. The Church Fathers searched for correspondences between events of the Old and New Testaments to show that Christ was the fufullment of the prophecies. First we must understand God's plan.

An essential part of the first Advent is, of course, the Fall of Man. The important thing here is that Adam disobeyed the command of God almost immediately; by eating of the fruit of the Tree of Knowledge he changed his own nature. The Fall became a kind of datum, a given fact, from which everything else follows; it made necessary the Incarnation, and this created a direct relationship between Adam and Christ which in turn shaped the understanding of the redemption and the manner of its working out.

St. Paul speaks of Christ as the Second Adam. (22) The Church Fathers also wrote on the significance of this relationsip. The fruit eaten by Adam brought death; to eat of Christ's body brings everlasting life. The necessity of the second Advent of God is the result of man's sin at the beginning of the world. (23) The disobedience of our first parents influences everything that his come after. The "Cursor" poet has God promise Adam a redeemer even as He expels him from Paradise:

> "Ful dere adam it sal be boght
> Till it be bett Þat Þu has wroght.
> Ta Þi wijf nu in Þi hand,
> For ȝe sal leue Þis lufsum land,   948
> In till Þe wreched world to gang;
> Þar Þu sal thinck Þi lijf ful lang,
> Lang pining Þare to drei,
> And siÞen dobil dede to dei.   952
> ȝe sal be flemed fra mi face,
> Bituix and i ȝou send mi grace,
> Þe oile of merci bos ȝou abide,
> I hete to send it ȝou sum tide." (24)   956

This is the beginning of all prophecies. Here is the first and basic principle of unity in the "Cursor Mundi".

Let us take one Old Testament personage and see how he is used to pre-figure Christ. Noah is rich in figural possibilities. Christ Himself refers to him in his teaching about the end of the world:

> Heaven and earth shall pass, but my words shall not pass…
> And as in the days of Noah, so shall also the Coming of the Son of man be. For as in the days before the flood, they were eating and drinking, marrying and giving in marriage, even till that day in which Noah entered the ark; And they knew not till the flood came, and took them all

away; so also shal the coming of the son of man be. (25)

St. Augustine generalized the correspondence into a formula for "Noah signifies Christ, and the ark signifies the Church." (26) Noah gathered his family into the ark and together they survived the first "ending" of the world, so in the final destruction, only the famiy of Christ will safely journey into eternal blessedness. The description of the coming of the Flood is given balance by the inclusion of the signs of Doom near the close of the vast work, thus giving the poem a balanced structure. The first ending of the world is described graphically – the sun and the moon hid their light, the earth quaked, the seas ran over the plains, beasts and men fled to the high ground until all the land was covered when the wolf and man, the lion and the deer, and the lady and her page swam side by side. The "Cursor" poet describes it thus:

Stormes ras on euer-ilk a side,	
Sun and mone leme gan hide,	
It mirked ouer all þis world wide,	1764
Þe rain it fell sua fell and fast.	
welles wer, þe bankes brast;	
Þe see to rise, þe erd to cleue,	
Þe springes gan ouer al vte dreue;	1768
Leuening fell wid thoner and rain	
Þe erd quok and dinned egain.	
Þe water wex vte ouer þe plaines,	
Þe bestis ran þen to montaynes,	1772
Men and wimmen ran þaim wid,	
Wele þai wend þar haf sum grid,	
All for noght þan suank a fote	
Quen þai cam þar was þar na bote.	1776
Thine on man ferli þat par suam	
Side bi side, bath wolf and man,	
Þe leon suam biside þe hert,	
Did na best til oþer vnquert,	1782

Þe sperhauk bi Þe starling,
Þar tent til oÞer nankines thing. (27)

The Flood is followed by the story of Abraham and Isaac in the "Cursor Mundi", which is one of the most significant tales in the whole of the Old Testament. The sacrifice of Isaac os a prefiguring of the crucifixion: it is a figure of a father sacrificing a son innocent of any crime. The figure is significantly different from its fulfillment, for the tragedy of the former is averted – God provides another offering in the place of Isaac – but the Son must die when His time comes. This last minute reprieve from death into life was likewise related by Medieval man to the Ressurection as a figure of Christ's triumph over death.

Even where the relationship or prefiguring is not stated directly, as in the incident in the "Cursor Mundi", knowledge of its existence could be assumed in a large portion of its audience. John Mirk, in a popular collection of sermons entitles "Festial", comments on the Sacrifice of Isaac in this manner:

> Then by Abraham ye schull
> Understonde Þe Fadyr of Heven,
> And by Isaac his sonne Ihesu
> Crist, Þe whech he spayrd not
> for no love Þat he had to him;
> but suffered Þe Gewes to lay Þe
> wode apon hym, Þat was Þe
> Crosse apon hys schuldres, and
> ladden hym to Þe mount of
> Calvary, and per dydyn hym
> On Þe autre of wode, Þat was
> Þe Crosse…Þen as pus
> was fygur of Crystys
> Passion longe or he wer borne,
> Right so Crist hymselfe Þis day
> yn Þe gospelle tolde to his

dyscypuls how he schuld be
scornyed, and betgn wyth
scorgys, and don to deth on
Þe crosse, and ryse Þe
Pryd day ageyne to byve. (28)

The poet does not oversimplify his work by making the figural connections explicit. They were such a common and accepted part of Medieval religious thought that his readers, who would have listened to many sermons on "figurative" exegesis year after year, would immediately comphrehend the relationship between episodes in the Old Testament which incidents in the life of Christ. Medieval man looked upon past history as being close to his own time. Though the figures of the Old Testament recede as we progress through the "Cursor Mundi", they are never completely lost from sight. Every moment is charged with memories of the past and expectations of the future; thereby we discover order and unity in the poem that tells several stories, each separate and apparently discontinuous, which span all human time. Like recurring chords in music, the figures and their fulfillment discover singleness in diversity. Form and meaning become one.

Chapter IV
The Use of Myth & Legend

Besides prophecy and fulfillment, which we briefly examined in the last chapter, the "Cursor Mundi" is knit together by the skillful use of myth and legend. This poem on the history of salvation has two binding strands of myth – the quest of Seth for the Oil of Mercy, and the story of the wands that in the course of time became the wood of Christ's cross.

With regard to its definition, let us quote Tillyard:

> "…I refer to the universal instinct of any human group, large or small, to invest, almost always unconsciously, certain stories or events or places or persons, real or fictional, with an uncommon significance; to turn them into instinctive centers of reference; to make among stories A, B, C, D, all roughly having the same theme or moral, one, and one only, the type. Made thus typical, the story becomes a communal possession, the agreed and classic embodiment of some way of thinking and feeling" (1).

In this sense of myth-making instinct is widespread. One can cite as an example the historical event of the Spartans resisting the Persians at Thermophylae as the myth common on the western world of heroic courage against desperate odds, or the story of Romeo and Juliet as that of young love ending in tragedy.

The two myths that we will examine in this chapter were

among the most prominent in Christendom during the Middle Ages. Medieval man saw a deeper significance in all acts of history: seemingly unconnected events were bound together in a common aim and direction. Events took on a new meaning as they illuminated each other. The idea of knitting together the myth of Seth's quest, and the story of Holy Rood with the account of Christ's Harrowing of Hell came from a sublime imaginative effort to realize dramatically the scriptural account of the central episode of the Christian creed.

It is a fact that the Bible is silent, or offers only a small amount of information concerning the details of Our Lord's early life, or what happened in the three days He was in the tomb before He rose from the dead on the first Easter morn. No wonder that pious imaginations were moved to supply the missing details and to link them with the prophets and legends such as the quest of Seth and the story of the Holy Rood. For the purpose of edification the legend-making processes were given full and free scope. On the other hand, early Christian heretics, particularly the gnostics, (2) felt the need of Gospel narratives to support their doctrines. Thus there grew up around the canonical Scriptures the collection of legends that comprise the so-called "Apocryphal New Testament". The non-canonical Gospels appeared as counterparts to the canonical Gospels of the four evangelists. Originally the word "apocryphal" did not mean that which is spurious or untrue, at least not in the minds of those who first employed it. According to the testimony of St. Augustine, some of the apocryphal writings were regarded as canonical. (3)

Even the most superficial readings of these Christian apocrychal writings, however, must disclose their inferiority to the Bible proper. They abound in accounts of alleged miracles which at time descend to absurdity. Nevertheless, the "Apocrypha are of the utmost importance for the Church historian since they supply valuable information about tendencies and customs which characterize the early church." (4) Accordingly, we possess in the apocryphal writings a picturesque and first hand source of Christian thought through the Middle Ages. Moreover, they represent the beginnings of Christian legend; they are intimately connected with Christian literature and art. The stained-glass windows of the Middle Ages would be indecipherable without reference to these.

Rev. M. R. James has given as an excellent appreciation of the place of apochypha in the history of Christian literature:

> People may still be heard to say, "After all, these Apocryphal Gospels and Acts, as you call them, are just as interesting as the old ones. It was only by accident or caprice that they were not put into the New Testament." The best answer to such loose talk has always been, and is now, to produce the writings, and let them tell their own story. It will very quickly be seen that these is no question of anyone's having excluded them from the New Testament: they have done that to themselves. "But, it may be said, if these writings are good neither as books of history, nor of religion, nor even as literature, why spend time and labour on giving them a vogue which on your own showing they do not deserve?" Partly, of course, in order to enable others to form a judgement on them, but that is not the whole case. The truth is that they must not be regarded only from the point of view which they claim for themselves. In almost every other aspect they have a great and enduring interest.
>
> If they are not good sources of history in one sense, they are in another. They record the imagination, hopes and fears of the men who wrote them; they show what was acceptable to the unlearned Christian of the first ages, what interested them, what they admired, what ideals of conduct they cherished for this life, what they thought they would find in the next. As folklore and romance, again, they are precious, and to the lover and student of medieval literature and art they reveal the source of no incon-

siderable part of his material and the solution of many a puzzle. They have, indeed, exercised an influence (wholly disproportionate to their intrinsic merits) so great and so widespread, that no one cares about the history of Christians though Christian art can possibly afford to neglect them. (5)

Material from the Apocryphal Gospels were combined with the Christian myths and legends to enrich and unify the history of salvation. The "Cursor" poet is the first writer in English to attempt to bring together most of the important items from these various sources. We shall now see how he uses the quest of Seth story to tighten his narrative of the Fall.

a) The Quest of Seth for the Oil of Mercy

The myth of the quest of Seth for the Oil of Mercy and the story of Holy Rood as it appears in the "Cursor Mundi" has been formed of elements from many sources. Certain episodes are derived from the Bible, others, from apocrypha and folklore. But despite the many episodes and diverse sources from which these episodes stem, the myth-legend has a kind of unity. It is here primarily a theological rather than an artistic or dramatic unity: it is a unity based on the concept that as man's fall was occasioned by a tree, so man's redemption was achieved through a tree. So effective is the unifying power of this concept that it conceals the fact that the myth has two entirely different origins. The first one from the so-called "Apocalypse of Moses" (6) deals with the Journey of Seth to Paradise to plead for the promised Oil of Mercy; the second deals with the history of the wood which later became to Cross. This second legend is carried on into Christian times with the well known continuation dealing with the discovery of the true Cross by Saint Helen in the fourth century.

Although the legends of the Oil of Mercy and the Holy Rood are not well known today, this was not the case during the

Medieval period:

> Despite the present unfamiliarity with the legend of Seth and the Holy Cross, it was enormously popular and widely dispersed in the Middle Ages, especially from the twelfth to the fifteenth centuries, appearing in dozens of versions not only in England, France and Germany, but in Italy, Holland, Russia, Bulgaria, Iceland, and elsewhere, and as late as the seventeenth century, making its appearance in Calderon's "Auto el Arbol del Mejor Frute" and "La Silbila del Oriente y Grain Reina de Saba." (7)

In England these legends were related in somewhat different versions in the following well-known works of the late Middle Ages: the "Travels" of Sir John Mandeville, (8) William Caxton's translation of the "Legenda aurea". (9) and Sir Thomas Malory's "Morte d' Arthur". (10) These are allusions to them in a number of English mystery plays; they appears in the dramatic literature of France and Germany, (11) and a complete version is dramatized in the Cornish "Origo Mundi" (12). In each of these works these two myths, as in the "Cursor Mundi", form part of a larger pattern. There are, however, a number of English texts devoted entirely to the narration of a fully developed Holy Cross legend: "The Holy Rode", the "Story of the Holy Rood", the "Canticum de Creatione", and "The Holy Cross". (13)

As we have said, this legend was represented not only in literature but also in art. It appeared at Troyes, in the windows of the church of Saint Martin es-Nignes, of Saint Panaleon, of Saint Madeleine, and of Saint Nizier. (14) It was frescoed on the walls of the Choir of Santa Croce in Florence by Agnolo Gaddi. (15) Pietro dela Francesca celebrated it in a series of frescoes in the Chapel of the Bocci in the Church of San Francesco at Arezzo. (16) It was painted on the walls of the Chapel of the Guild of the Holy Cross in the Church of the Trinity at Stratford-upon-Avon. (17) One of the most complete pictorial representations of the legend of Seth

and the Holy Cross appears in the Dutch work, "Boec van den houte" (1483). There is a series of sixty-four wood cuts depicting the legend from Adam giving instruction to Seth to Saint Helen's finding of the Cross. (18)

William Meyer, the nineteenth century German scholar, lists a total of fifty works which use the Seth – Holy Cross story during the late Medieval period. (19)

Investigation into the origins of the Seth legend reveals that the quest of Adam's son for the Oil of Mercy was not originally connected with the legend of the Cross but considerably antedated Christianity. In the form in which it appears in the "Cursor Mundi", some elements are missing and others have been added, but the core is unmistakably an ancient Jewish apocryohal tale. Although of Jewish origin, the earliest extant version of the Seth legend is in Greek. (20) The part of this apocryphal story which concerns us here, the journey of Seth to Paradise, may be briefly summarized as follows

> At the age of 930 Adam falls ill and bids all his sons to come to him. Seth offers to get the fruit of Paradise, but Adam refuses. Instead he bids Eve and Seth to go to Paradise and pray God to give them "of the tree out of which the oil floweth." They are to put earth on their heads, as a sign of penitence. On the way they encounter a wild beast, whose ferocity is dispelled by the "image of God" in Seth. When they arrive, God sent the archangel Michael to refuse Seth "the Oil of Mercy", but promises him that it shall be given to the holy people at the end of time. (21)

The form in which the Seth legend passed into Western European literature is the Latin Version of the "Apocalypse of Moses", known as the "Vitae Adae et Evae". (22) Of particular interest at this early stage in the legend's development is the object of Seth's quest, "the Oil of Mercy". The form that it will take is not made clear in the old Jewish original tale.

The first known instance of a Christian adoption of the Seth legend is in the apocryphal "Gospel of Nicodemus". (23) Originally composed in Greek in about the fourth century, it was early translated into Latin and then the vernacular. There is a thirteenth century Middle English version of the "Gospel of Nicodemus". (24) The central idea of the work is the delivery of the righteous Old Testament patriarchs and prophets from hell. It describes how Seth, at the time of the Harrowing of Hell, told the patriarchs of his journey to Paradise; he then announced that Christ would bring the promised Oil of Mercy. This Christianization of the Seth legend was later inserted into the 'Vitae Adae et Evae". As yet Seth was unconnected with the legend of the wood of the cross, but an important link had been established: Seth and his quest had been absorbed into Christian legend. This borrowing from "The Gospel of Nicodemus" of the specific prophecy of Christ's coming was henceforth to be a constant element in the Seth story.

The merging of the Seth and the rood-tree legends seems to have occurred first with an interpolation into he "Vitae Adae et Evae" of a Holy Cross legend. (25) The earliest extant version which relates the combined Seth and Holy Cross legends is Johannes Beleth's "Rationale divinorum officiorum", written in Medieval Latin in about 1171. In Beleth's account, Adam sends Seth and Eve to Paradise and Seth returns with a branch from the tree of knowledge, which he plants. Another early version is that as Adam and Eve were leaving Paradise, he broke from a tree a branch that he used as a staff.

One of the most widely known Medieval versions of the Seth story occurs in Peter Comestor's "Historia Scholastica". This version, which may have been known to the "Cursor" poet, contains several details omitted from some later retellings of the legend. For example, Seth and Eve got to Paradise for the Oil of Mercy, but they receive instead of the oil, a branch which has three leaves on it. In this version, Adam was buried at Calvary. Another new element is the detail that the blood of Christ fell from the cross upon the skull of Adam. (26)

In these early combined versions the rood-tree legends were of the twig type; at the next stage, the seed type was to prevail. The most highly developed and most widely influential form of this later seed type of legend is a Latin text of the thirteenth century, to which Meyer gives the name "Legende". (27) Its widespread popularity is attested to by its considerable number of manuscripts in Latin and its translations and adaptions into most European languages. (28) This "Legende" us a bold and elaborate tale, a fitting climax to the development of the legends of Seth and the Holy Cross. Here several innovations appear which were to become incorporated in almost every subsequent version, including the "Cursor Mundi". There are the withered grass trail which Adam and Eve made when they left Paradise and which Seth used as a guide on his quest for the Oil of Mercy; there are the three visions which Seth saw through the gates of Paradise; and finally there are the three apple seeds which he is given instead of the Oil of Mercy. The "Cursor" poet may have used the "Legende" as a direct source, or merely depended on one of the retellings of the legend as found in works such as the French poet, Herman of Valenciennes' poem bearing in the different manuscripts, the varying titles: "Li Livres de la Bible", "Histoire de la Bible", "Bible de Sapience", "Roman de Sapience." (29)

No matter how interesting a tracing of the sources of Seth legend may be, our primary concern is to see how the "Cursor" poet handles his material in order to achieve a tight unified narrative of salvation.

Let us now turn to the "Cursor Mundi" and examine the way in which the poet weaves the quest for the Oil of Mercy into the early sections of his poem. Within the larger drama of the "Cursor Mundi", which tells the story of a man from creation of the world to the Judgement Day, this myth forms a kind of subplot: its episodes are not related as a unit but are interwoven throughout the work. The relevant parts of the quest of Seth may be summarized as follows:

> When Adam is about to die, he bids his son Seth go to Paradise for the Oil of Mercy. The path will be apparent

since, as Adam and Eve left Paradise their feet destroyed the grass, and no vegetation has ever grown there. Seth is refused the Oil of Mercy, but is granted three glimpses of Paradise. In the first he beholds a dry tree; in the second, an adder twined about the trunk; in the third, a newborn baby in the top of the tree. He is told that the dry tree and the serpent represent the sin of man and that the baby is Christ, who will be the Oil of Mercy. Seth receives three kernels of the tree of life and plants them in the mouth of his dead father. From the kernels three trees grow – a cedar, a cypress, and a pine – and remain growing in the Vale of Hebron until the time of Moses.

The first mention of the "Oil of Mercy" in the "Cursor Mundi" is when God passes judgment on Adam and Eve because of their transgression. He says that they will be exiled from His face till he sends the Oil of Mercy at some future date:

> "Ful dere adam it sal be boght
> Till it be bett þat þu has wrought.
> Ta þi wijf nu in þi hand,
> For ȝe sal leue þis lufsum land,   948
> In till þe wreched world to gang;
> Þar þu sal thinck þi lijf ful lang,
> Lang pining þare to drei,
> And siþen dobil dede to dei.   952
> ȝe sal be flemed fra mi face,
> Bituix and i ȝou send mi grace,
> Þe oile of merci bos ȝou abide,
> I hete to send it ȝou sun tide." (24)   956

Adam then asks how he can get reconciliation: God does not explain what he means by the Oil of Mercy.

After the "Cursor" poet has dealt with the story of Cain and Abel, he returns to the Oil of Mercy motif. Adam, who is now more than nine hundred years old, (31) has grown weary of life because of his endless years of toil. He tells his son Seth he must go to the angel guarding the gates of Paradise and bid for the Oil of Mercy. He gives direction to Seth on how to find the way there:

    "ȝeis," he said, "i sal þe tell and say,
    Hugat þu sal ta þi right way.
    Tilward þe est end of þe dale,
    A grene gate find þu sale, (32)   1252
    In þat way sal yu find forsoth
    Þi moþer and myn oþer broþer sloth.
    Foluand thoru þat griss greene,
    Þat euer has ben syden sene,   1256
    Þar we cam wendand as vnwise,
    Quen we war put fra paradise
    Vnto þis worldes wreched slade,
    Þer i mi-self first was made; (33)   1260

Seth must go to Paradise, along a grass-green path, towards the east of the dale, following the track left by Adam and Eve. His father wants to know of the angel at the gate, when he may leave this world, and whether he shall have the promised Oil of Mercy:

    Þu sal him say i am vnfere,
    For i haue liuede so mani a ȝere,   1268
    Ay in strijf and soru stadd,
    Þat wid mi lijf I wax all mad,
    Þu prai him þat word me send,
    Quen i sal fra þis world wend.   1272
    Anoþer errand sal þar be,
    Þat he wild send me word bi þe,
    For i sal haue it vte in hey,
    Þat me was hight þe oile of merci,   1276
    Þat time þat I left paradijs,
    And left it thoru mi folis. (34)

The search for the Oil of Mercy, introduced in this important passage helps to maintain the tight thread of narrative unity to almost the end of the poem. This is also a clear statement by Adam that he hoped to be given forgiveness and to receive the Oil of Mercy, which in another version of the legend is referred to as the "oil of life – that medicine is to man and wife." (34) Adam admits his great sin of disobedience but prays that he had now earned some pity. Seth sets out on his quest without delay and finds no difficulty in following his father's instructions. He arrives at the gates of Paradise the same day, and tells the angel stationed there the object of his quest, and asks when Adam can expect the long awaited Oil of Mercy:

> Seth went forth widuten nay,
> To paradis Þat ilke day,   1284
> Þe sloth he fand Þat gan him wise,
> Till Þat he cam at paradise.
> Quen he Þarof had a sight,
> He was al dredand of Þat light;   1288
> Suilk a light as he sau Þare,
> A brinand fir he wend it ware,
> He blissed him as his fader badd,
> And went forth was nought radd.   1292
> Þis angel at Þe ȝate he fand,
> And asked him of his errand.
> Seth Þan sett him spell onende,
> And teld him quarfor Þat he was send,   1296
> Teld him of hijis faderis care,
> Als he him taght, and ȝe herd are,
> To send him word quen he sal dei,
> Langer to liue may he noght drei;   1300
> And quen Þat god him had tight,
> Þe oyle of merci Þat he him hight. (35)

The angel does not give an immediate answer to Seth, but

The Narrative Unity of the Cursor Mundi

commands him to put his head within the gate of Eden, and to note whatever he sees therein. Seth did as he was bidden, and saw more marvels than tongue could tell. The meads were decked with gay herbs and trees, diffusing all around most delightful perfumes. In the middle of the land was a bright, shining well, out of which flowed four streams as Tyson, Fison, Tigri and Eufrate. Above the well there stood a large tree with many branches, but without bark or leaves, like an aged dead tree. Seth supposed that the tree stood thus bare, like the grass on the way to Eden, on account of his parents' sin. He turns to the angel and describes what he has seen.

When he looks through the gates a second time, he observes that a serpent, all naked and without skin, was embracing the ancient bare tree. On looking a third time, Seth sees, to his amazement, that the tree has changed. It now reaches to the sky, while a new-born child, wrapped in swaddling clothes, lies crying at the top. The root of the tree went down into the uttermost ends of hell, and there he saw the soul of his brother Abel:

>Þe pepinis war don vnder his tong,
>Þar ros of þaim þre wandis ȝong,
>And sone an elne hight þai were,
>Þai stod þan still and wex no mare.   1420
>Mani a ȝere elike al grene,
>Halines on þaim was sene,
>Still þai stod ay, þa wandes thre,
>Fra adanu time vnto noee;   1424
>Fra noee quen þe flode ras,
>Till habraham þat hali was,
>Fra Abraham time still stod þai
>Till moyses þat gaue þe lay;   1428
>Euer stod þai still in ane,
>widuten waxing or wane. (40)

The pippins which had been placed under the root of Adam's tongue after a time began to grow, and three small wands grew up, and stood "without waxing or waning" from Adam's death until the time of Moses. Each grew separately by itself out of the same root, and was of an ell in height and no more. The poet shows his art as a storyteller by selecting those details from this myth that will appeal to his readers. His account of Seth's quest is some two hundred lines in length. It is not so long as to unbalance his narrative. The transition from the legendary material dealing with the origins of the Holy Cross to the description of Adam's offspring is smooth; the poet declares that he will give no more of the story at this point:

> Na more of Þa wandis nou
> Bot a stori sal i rede 3ou. (41)   1432

We have now to consider the second leading myth, that of the Holy Rood.

b) The Legend of the Holy Rood

To the Medieval Christian, the cross on which the Savior died for the redemption of Man was made of no ordinary wood. Following Saint Helen's discovery of the true cross, fragments had been dispersed throughout Christendom and had become objects of veneration and speculation. From those two impulses of the medieval imagination, curiosity and credulity, a body of legend developed about the wood of the cross. Miracles were attributed to the relics whose wonder-working power was linked with the cross.

The legend of the wands that in time grew into the wood from which Christ's cross was made starts in most of its versions in the days of Moses. The "Cursor" poet was one of the first writers in English to combine the myths of the Oil of Mercy and of the Holy Cross into one organic whole. His skillful handling of the various threads of these legends strengthens the narrative unity of the whole poem.

The earliest extant Middle English version of the Cross-legend is "The Holy Rood-Tree", which dates from the twelfth century. (42) This version commences thus:

> Here beings to be told concerning the tree of which our lord suffered for the salvation of all mankind, how it first began to grow. We heard it told by a certain wise man that Moses, when he went from Egypt over the Red Sea with the Israelitish people, when he delivered them from the captivity under Pharoh, came to the place which is named Quinquaginta Fineas, and there rested two nights. During the first night he rested there, on the selfsame spot on which he lay, there grew three rods, the one was at his head, a second at his right side, and a third at his left. (43)

Napier considers this to be the oldest surviving form of the rood-tree legend in Europe. (44)

Most of the elements of the story of the wands that are consistent with the "Cursor" poet's purpose of linking the Fall of Man to the Redemption of Man by Christ on the Cross are included in his version of the legend. The relevant sections that appear in the "Cursor Mundi" may be summarized as follows:

> The trees that have grown from the seed planted in Adam's mouth are uprooted by Moses and become the wands with which he sweetens the water of Marah and brings forth water from a rock.

> David recovers the wands from the desert, which are now united to form a single staff. With it he changes the colour and shape of some Ethiopians. The miraculous staff is replanted and grows into a tree.

> Later Solomon attempts to use it in building his temple, but in whatever the tree is cut, it is always too long or too short. Perceiving its miraculous power, Solomon had the tree placed in the temple.

One day a lady named Maximilia accidentally sits on the tree, and, when it bursts into flames, she is inspired to prophecy. The Jews, hearing that Christ will die upon this wood, put Maximilia to death and hurl the tree into a pit.

Miracles are performed until Jews remove the tree and placed over a stream to serve as a bridge. The holy nature of the wood is announced by the Sibyl, who refuses to walk on it and instead wades through the brook barefoot.

At the time of the Crucifixion, a cross is made of the tree. The cross, however, cannot be lefted by any except Christ, since it was destined for Him. By His dying on it He becomes the redeemer, or the Oil of Mercy, for mankind.

These episodes appear at the appropriate place in the "Cursor Mundi", tightening the structure of the poem.

The Moses episode of the Rood-tree legend in the "Cursor Mundi" begins with a dream of Moses, for after the Isrealites had escaped from Egypt by crossing the Red Sea, they came into the vale of Hebron where Adam had been buried. As they were suffering greatly from thirst, the Jewish leader, harassed by the problem of finding water for the large host, retires for the night and in sleep sees a wonderful vision of the wands:

> Moyses Þat niht in sleping lay,   6316
> Þat niht he ȝede and tok his rest,
> In sleping he lat in Þat forest,
> Quen he on morn him lokid bi
> He sau Þat him thought ferli,   6320
> At his heued sau he stand
> waxin of cypris, a wand;
> Apon his left hand loked he,
> AnoÞer he sau of cyder tre;   6324
> And quan he lokid on his riht hand,
> Of Pine tre Þe third he fand; (45)

Moses had the same vision of the wands on the two succeeding nights, and realizes that they must be a sign of some wonder.

At this point the poet ties the wands in with the Holy Trinity, on which the whole work is based –

> Þarfor Þis werke i wil found
> On a selcuth stedfast grund,
> Þat es Þe hali trinite. (46)

This reference on the Trinity also links up with the opening of the "Cursor Mundi" proper, which describes the characteristics of the Trinity. Here the poet suggests that the sun, at once round, hot and light, is an emblem of God in the Blessed Trinity. He goes on to explain that the body of the sun is similar to the Father, the light to the Son, and its heat to the Holy Ghost, which proceeds from both the Father and the Son:

> Þe suns bodi Þat i neuen
> Bi-takins Þe fader self of heuen,   304
> And bi Þi light Þat es lastand
> It es Þe sone Þu vnderstand,
> And bi Þe hete Þu vnderstand so,
> Þe hali gast comes of Þaim to. (47)   309

Moses, in keeping with the Medieval habit of making all history, in a sense, contemporary, knows all about the Trinity:

> "Selcuth thing," he said, "wid-in
> Es closid in Þa wandis thrin."   6320
> Þa wandis takin parsonis thre,
> And a-fold god in vnite.
> Þan he drou Þaim vp at Þe first,
> Widuten ani skade or brist,   6324
> And quiles Þai in Þat wildernes ware,
> Þa wandis ay wid him he bare. (48)

Realizing that the wands betokened the Trinity, Moses took them up without breaking them, and carried them wherever he went in the wilderness. The Isrealites found water in the desert, but it was bitter as brine, quite undrinkable. The wands, however, when placed in this water made it fit to drink:

> Siþen þai fand þat frith widine,
> water bitter as ani brin, 5348
> As it war brine sua was it bitteri,
> To drine it ne was þaim neuer þe better.
> Bot quan þa wandis war in don,
> Þe water wex suete als sone, 5352
> Þa watris þat sua foule stanc,
> Of suetter neuer nan þai bifor drane. (49)

By means of these wands, Moses also healed the sick, and performed numerous other miracles. And when he climbed Mount Sinai where he received the Ten Commandments from God, he hid the wands in the ground. These miraculous wands remained always in leaf and flower. They also emitted the most pleasant perfume. This is how the "Cursor" poet put it:

> For na drie ne for na wate,
> Ne changid þai neuer þair state,
> Bot euer þai held lijf and flour,
> Sauirand wid a suete sauuer. (50) 6368

The poet later on mentions that Moses used these wands, when on another occasion the Israelites were without water in the desert, to hit the rock. The rock broke and out burst a stream, sufficient for all the needs of the wandering host:

> And vte as a brok it brast þe strand,
> Þar had þai water in wilderness land,
> Plente for men, to fhote and hand. (51)

Moses never lets the magic wands out of his possession until he had the ark and tabernacle built. He then places them in this holy place:

> Þan he tok vp Þa wandies thrin,
> And for to kepe did Þaim Þar-in,   6664
> For-to bere to ilka stede,
> QueÞer so he Þee folk wild lede. (52)

However, just before he dies, he takes the wands from the ark, and plants them in a hidden place, where they remain until the time of King David. This is how the "Cursor Mundi" concludes the section on Moses:

> Bot moyses, right-wis of rede,
> For-gat he noght, ar he war dede,
> To sett his hali wandis thre
> In a stede he fand priue,   6940
> Þar Þai greu neyder less ne mare,
> Bot euer bifor as Þai ware,
> Right to king dauid dais,
> Þat ledd his folk in gode lays,   6944
> Þat thoru warning of godes sande,
> Broght Þaim to his aun lande. (53)

The inclusion of the Moses and the wands episode helps to unify the Redemption story, looking towards the passion of Christ. It permits the "Cursor" poet to refer back to the beginning of the poem to the section on the Trinity and as we shall see forward to the crucifixion.

    The next time that the wands appear is in the reign of King David. Here the "Cursor" poet devotes one thousand lines of his religious epic (54) to the history of the tree that was to become Christ's cross. He commences by describing how an angel appeared to David in a dream. The angel said that God wanted King

David to cross the Jordon into the country where Moses was buried, and that there he would find the three wands that Moses had carried with him for years:

>Þu sal find Þa wandis Þare,
>Þat moyses oft wid him bare,
>Of cydyr, pyne, and of cypress,
>Þar war Þai sett thoru moyses. (55)   8008

The angel then goes on to explain to the King in his dream that no one can say what great virtue and grace are in these wands whose very shadow his miraculous powers. He says:

>Es na man for-soth can say
>Of how grett vertu and grace er Þai,
>Nor na manes tung can say ne mele   8024
>Quat Þai sal bere of soulis hele;
>Of Þaim Þu sal haue a gret vauntage,
>Bath to Þe and Þi barnage;
>Qua may him rest onder Þaim oumbery,   8028
>Es Þar na thing Þat may him cumber.
>Haue god day, for nou wend I, (56)

Here we have a foreshadowing of the wise judgements of Solomon, who was to hold court under the shadow of this wonderful tree. David, according to this version of the legend, without question crosses the river Jordan with his folk and finds the wands. He had no trouble in recognizing them as they are of one height, alike, though different with the three heads growing from one stem. The King knelt to kiss them before drawing them out of the ground without breaking them. David then held them up, and the people saw them sine with light. This shining light as a motif found in many of the Medieval lives of the saints and also appears in the romances of the age. For example of the latter, Havelok the Dane shone while he was asleep thus showing his royal blood.

The Narrative Unity of the Cursor Mundi

This episode of the "Cursor Mundi" has several of the characteristics that we associate with saints' lives or even romances. This is how the poet introduces this light:

> And quen þe king cam ner þas tres,
> Honurd and kist þaim on his knes;
> He drow þaim vp, soft i-nogh,
> widuten breking of any bow.   8044
> Quen þe king þaim had vte-tan,
> His host þaim honurd, euerilk-an,
> Þe king þaim held vp in þair sight,
> A lem schan of þa branches bright,   8048
> Þat all his ost miht se þa branches bright,
> Þat all his ost miht se þat leuen
> Hou it rahut vp into heuen. (57)

The "Cursor" poet selects four miracles of the many that appear in various versions of the legend, for inclusion in his work. All four occur on King David's journey back to Jerusalem. The first deals with a rich man who has been ill for a ling time and had lost all hope of recovery. The moment he sees the wands, however, he is made hale and sound. A short time later, the King's procession met four rich "Saracens", black and misshapen, their mouth in their breast, brows hanging about their ears and eyes in their forehead. They were four monstrous creatures that hardly looked like human beings at all. The poet appears to delight in making them as misshapen as possible; his description is vivid:

> Foure sarazins wid þe king gan mwte,   8072
> Blac and bla as led þai ware,
> Mekil riches wid þaim þai bare,
> Þat saw man neuer bifore þat oure,
> Sua frawar[d] schapin creatoure.   8076
> Of þair blac hew it was seleuth,
> And in þair brestes þai bar þair muth,

> Lang and side Þair broues wern
> And recched al a-boute Þair'ern   8080
> Þair muthes wid, Þair eyen brad,
> Ful wondererful was Þair facis mad!
> In Þair forhefd was Þair sight,
> Loke ne miht Þair sight,   8084
> Loke ne miht Þai nought vpright;
> Þair armys hari, wid harplid hide,
> war sett til elboues in Þair side,
> Crumplid knes, and bouch on bacl (58)   8088

The description of these four strangers from Ethiopia is similar to some of the wonders that appear in Medieval accounts of foreign countries. The four prophesy that Christ will die on the rood-tree:

> Pyne on Þat tre suffer he sall,
> Þe king of blis for his folk all. (59)   8100

They request to see the wands, declaring they have the power to heal them. They devoutly knell and kiss the wands and immediately their skin becomes white and their shape set right. These foriegners can foretell the part the wands will play in the redemption of mankind:

> Of Þaim sal rise vr raunsun,
> And of all vr sinnes pardun,
> To Þaim Þat merci for Þair sinne
> Cries to iesu, of dauid kinne; (60)   8122

It is this from these unexpected lips that David is told that his descendant will ransom men and save them from sin.

The third miracle on the return from the wilderness is the cursing of a leperous hermit who had had a dream that the light from the wands will restore him to good health. This proves to be so. The final miracle of the journey is when the waters of the

Jordan River divides so that King David, bearing the miraculous wands, walks across dry-shod.

> Þe king went forth ful sone onan,
> Til he com a-gayn to flum iordan.
> He tok þa wandes in his hand,
> Þe strem still bigan to stand,   8188
> It stod þe folk on ayder side
> Þe kinges passage fot to bide.
> Quen þai war pascid ouer þe strand,
> And all comen vp-on þe toþer land,   8192
> Witt ȝe wele þai war ful glad;

These four wonderful stories would have appealed to the "Cursor" poet's contemporaries.

On returning to Jerusalem, King David placed the wands in a cistern, with men and lamps to guard them during the night. On the morrow he intended to take them in procession into the city and replant them in his own orchard. Overnight, however, the took root so that no one could pull them out:

> Þai rested þaim þat niht and bade,
> Of þe wandis gret los þai made;   8204
> Aboute was þaim þe king ful ȝerne,
> He putt þaim in-to a cysterne,
> And did he siden þaim laumpis liht,
> And sett men þaim to kepe all niht,   8208
> Þe quiles þe king him went to slepe.
> Bot god þat al has for to kepe,
> Þat all for-lokis in his sight,
> His will widstande has nan na miht,   8212
> Es na-thing þat may for-barre
> His wille þat bifore es sua war,
> He þat sua mihti es and wise
> He did þa wandis for to rise,   8224

> In þat cystener þe rotis fest,
> Sua depe þa rotis samen kest,
> Þat miht na man þaim þeden winne
> Widuten breche, for any gynne. (62)   8220

David took this as a sign that they should ne left alone and ordered that a Wall and garden were to be made around the growing rood-tree. Every year for thirty years David put a silver hoop around the tree;

> Quen it was closid aboute, þat tre,
> A siluer cerkil sone naylede he,   8242
> Þat was þe stauin for to strenthe,
> And knaw þe wax of gret and lenthe.
> Suilkin serklis sett he sere,
> Thritti winter, ilka ȝere,   8246
> And did an to, i ȝou say,
> Euer quen he tok anoþer away. (63)

When King David's son, Solomon, comes to cut down the tree to use as the main spar for the great temple, the thirty silver circles are made into coins that are placed into the temple treasury. They remain there until they are used to pay Judas. This is how the poet puts it:

> At þe temple for þis resun,
> Þai er wid tresur in commun,
> Ne wat þai neuer þan spend,
> Til þat þai war iudas bikend,   8840
> To him þan war þai taght and tald,
> Quen he for þaim his lauerd sald. (64)

Undoubtedly the "Cursor" poet knew of other stories about the thirty pieces of silver that commence with Abraham, and appear and re-appear according to legend throughout salvation history. Nevertheless, he must have decided that the Seth-Holy Rood sequence would better fit his purpose by giving dramatic unity to his work.

It was while King David was sitting under the tree of life that he had the inspiration to build a magnificent temple to God in which to keep the sacred ark, the tables of law, Aaron's rod, manna and the golden oil of the propitiatory sacrifice:

Quen he had made his orisoun,	8264
Vnder þat tre he sett him doun,	
He thought þan was suilk a lording,	
A temple thoght he make on hight,	
In þe worschip of god all-miht;	8268
Fer and depe he him bithoght,	
Hou þat þis temple suld be wroght,	
For to kepe in þair ser relike,	
Þat he miht saue in his kingrike;	8272
Þat was, þat hali arke þai bare	
Aboute, wid all þair sayntuare,	
Þat es to say, þe tablis tuin,	
Þat þe ten comandementis war in,	8276
Þat god wrat wid his aun hand;	
I, and þar-in was aaron-es wand,	
Þar bar þe fruit þou it war drie;	
And of manna als a partye;	8280
Þe gylden oyle of þe propiciatory,	
To cherubynes, als sas þe story.	

While the King was thus thinking, an angel from God came and sat on a bough of the tree of life and told him that God knows of his desire to build the temple in His honour, and that it should be finished during the reign of his son, Solomon. Thus David was denied the joy of completing the temple, for, as the angel reminded him, he was a man of blood. The "Cursor" poet does not mention that King David composed his penitential psalms under this tree, only that he prophesied the coming of Christ and that he made the Psalter:

> Þis ilk it was, king dauy,
> Þat mekil spae of prophesy,
> Of cristes birth ful lang biforn,
> Þat of a mayden suld be born.   8524
> Þat mayden of his aune sede
> Was getyn, in bokis as we rede,
> And vr lauerd bi-for him high[t],
> Of him suld spring Þat all suld right.   8528
> Þis ilke dauid Þe sauter made,
> Is ress ouer-all Þis world brande. (66)

But the poet foes treat in some etail the wonderful childhood of David's son, Solomon. He commences by saying that no child ever loved "clergy" more than Solomon and that he soon mastered the Seven Liberal Arts, which was the basic curriculum of the Medieval university:

> Þis child was sone sett to bok,
> And clergy wele he vnder-tok,   8426
> For all his herte he gaf to lare,
> Might neuer child loue clergy mare.
> Thoru Þe grace of god of heuen,
> Sone he coude Þe artis seuen. (67)   8440

The young Solomon loved the holy tree, and often sat under it, learning many wise things under his shadows. The poet says that Solomon put the learning he recieved under its shadows, consolidated them into the three books of Ecclesiastes, Proverbs, and Canticles:

> For vnder Þe vmber of Þat tre,   8452
> Þe king of thinges lered he,
> Bath and of tres, grisses fele,
> Quilk war Þair vertus lele,
> For quatkin euil ilkan miht gayn,

> Quer-so þai grew in wode or playn; 8456
> And queþer þe medicin of bote,
> Funden be in cropp or rote.
>
> Of lare he lerid vnder þat tre,
> Þan made he gode bokis thre, 8460
> And dohutyli he þaim vndid,
> Wid saumplis of tres and griss imid.
> Þe first bok, widuten les,
> Men it callis ecclesiastises, 8464
> Þat spekis mast, widuten wand,
> Hou fals þis world es forto fand.
> Of prouerbis es þe toþer bok,
> Þat leris man him vmbiloke 8468
> Agaynes þis he au him for to lede.
> Þe third bok, efter þa tua,
> Þe quilk me clepis cantica,
> A notful bock in hali writ, 8470
> Þe bok of loue men clepis itt,
> For of þat loue it spekis mast
> Bituix manes saule and þe hali gast. (68)

As this point in the narrative, the "Cursor" poet gives a brief summary of the poem so far:

> Bituix and he quam bar marie,
> Henge þer-on his folk to bie,
> Be barntem of alde adam,
> Þat thoru a bitt broght all in blam, 8500
> An applis bitt, bath man and wijf,
> Þat thoru a bitt, bath man and wijf,
> Þat tre was dede, þis sal be lijf.
> And written es in parchemin, 8504
> Þat it cam vte of þat pepyn,
> Þat wrecched adam fel fra,

> And broght him seluen, in mekil wa:
> For sua bigan þe crois, i wis,   8508
> Of iesu crist vr king of blis. (69)

Thus the poet enhances the artistic unity of his long religious poem by showing clearly its continuity. The occasion of the recapitulation is the quoting of the gold inscription on the marble stone at the foot of the aging tree of life. This is what the inscription says:

> "sum-time þat men suld se
> Godd him-seluen reyne in þat contre,   8486
> Þat plantid was bituix þa floures,
> Þar þe stremis held þair cours.
> Wele i wate neuer es it wan,
> Of flour ne fruit þat it has tan,   8490
> And in þis time suilk fruit suld geue,
> Þat all his freindes þar-of suld leue;
> Ne of þat fruit suld na man bite,
> Þat he ne suld lone it als tite." (70)   8494

The poem then returns to his account of the life of King Solomon. Once, while sitting under the miraculous tree, Solomon in a vision was offered by an angel the choice between three gifts – strength, riches, or wisdom. He chose the last. He gave judgement between the two women who claimed the same baby while he sat under the sacred tree.

At the time when the temple was being built, the tree began to wither, and people said it was dying of old age:

> Nou bigan it to wax ald;
> Ilk a man said, þat it sie,
> Þat it for elde bigan to drey,   8768
> And semed wele it wild ne mare,
> Þat men suld it hald in are, (71)

Meanwhile the workmen, who were building the temple, had been seeking far and wide for a suitable "mayster sperr" for the edifice. They asked leave of Solomon to cut down the aging sacred tree in the royal orchard. The King seeing no other course open to him, gave his consent. But when hewn and lifted into its place, it would not fit because it was too short, and after the workmen had tried in vain for three days, the beam from the sacred tree was laid in the temple together with the thirty silver rings, which were afterwards given to Judas. The power of the wood to change its length is a motif that occurs in other Medieval legends. St. Erkenwalk, first bishop of London (ca. 686), according to the Venerable Bede, on one occasion lengthens a piece of timber with the aid of his sister St. Ethelburga. (72) The same type of incident also appears in the "Apocryphal Gospel of Thomas", (73) which is included in the "Cursor Mundi". (74) The poet declares that nothing was ever made of the wood from the tree of life except Christ's cross:

> Þat tre Þat ful richely,
> Was in Þat temple don to ly,
> Was Þar neuer of made oght,   8848
> Tille Þat Þe crois Þar-of was wrought. (75)

The workmen found a suitable beam as the master spar of the temple on the first day of looking which was thought to be miraculous. When the temple was blessed, the wood lay in it in peace.

The next episode that the "Cursor" poet selects from the mass of legendary material surrounding the Holy Rood deals with the efforts of a priest called Cyril to destroy the sacred tree. After Solomon's time "Cirillus" came with five hundred men and tried to take the holy tree away, but it could not be moved. The episode opens with these lines:

> Quen Þat Þe temple haluid wes,
> Þe tre euer it lay stille in pes,   8868
> Mani it wald haue done a-way,
> Bot miht Þai noght, still it lay.

> And efter salamones day
> Þer cam a preist, was of Þat lay,   8872
> Þer-to fiue hundred men he leed,
> Bot Þai miht neuer stir it of stedd; (76)

The priest then attempts to chop it up, but no sooner had he begun when the beam burst into flame,

> wid ax he wald haue cut it Þan,
> all-to sone he it bigan   8876
> vt of Þat tre it brast a blass,
> Þat brint Þaim all in Þat place,
> Þat quie cam nan of Þaim ham: (77)

The blaze burnt the large group so that none of them returned to their homes alive. The "Cursor" poet, in a few lines, had made a stark, vivid story out of the legend surrounding the priest Cyril. In a dozen lines he has given us the essence of the legend.

In the succeeding section, the author has drawn upon material which tells of Maximilla, "the first Christian Martyr". This episode reads like a selection from one of the large cycles of legendary lives of the saints. Once a lady called Maximilla came to the temple to worship and pray; she sat down unaware on the sacred beam whereupon her clothes commenced to burn. The she began to prophesy,

> apon Þat tre suld hing
> Þat lauerd of helle, Þat blissful king,
> Iesu crist of maydin born,
> To saue Þe world Þat was for-lorn. (78)   8908

She predicted that the Jews would make a cross from the wood. When the Jews heard her call upon Jesus Christ, they were exceedingly angry, because he had slandered their God by the mention of a new one, so they turned against her and beheaded her without delay. An angel carried Maximilla's sould up to heaven in sight of all the people, saying that she was a Christian which infuriated the Jews. I quote the final lines of the episode:

> Sent Þan was an angel þare,
> And vp to heuen hir saule bare,
> In hir folk hir alder siht,
> And said þat cristian scho   8920
> Þar-for war þe iuus wrath,
> Þat name to here was þaim ful lath.
> Þis woman was first þat men wist,
> Þat martird was fore iesu crist.   8924

The hatred and violence of the Jews to this prophetess is a foreshadowing of their action against the early Christians, and may have been included by the "Cursor" poet for this reason. That is to show that sections of the chosen race were set against Christ, even before His birth.

The Jews attempted to get rid of the Holy Rood by throwing it into a fish-pond ("piscyna probatyca"). (80) But God sent angels from heaven to stir the water of the pool, and as a result it was endowed with miraculous powers of healing. The poet does not mention the name of the pool. It is similar to the one at Bethzatha that is mentioned in the New Testament. (81) The healing power of certain objects thrown into water is a recurring motif in the legendary lives of the saints.

The following section relates that the Jews, angered again by the miracle which occurred in the "piscyna probatyce", dragged the wood from the pond and made a bridge across the brook known as Siloe. (82) Meyer ascribes this episode to Jacobus de Voragine's "Legenda aurea", but the account in Johannes Beleth's "Rationale divinorum officiorum" (ca. 1170) is essentially the same and considerable earlier. (83). The Jews hoped that sinful men's feet would tread out the virtue of the tree:

> "If þat ani vertu be
> Of olines widin þis tre,   8940

wid sinful menes fete," said Þai,
"wid ganging sal be done away." (84)

Thus, the tree lay until the Sibyl (85) came from afar to hear Solomon's wisdom. (86) Though Sibyl will not cross by the bridge made of the Holy Rood, but after kneeling down in honour to it, she waded through the stream. She also prophesied that the tree was a token of judgement that will come to all men.

This is how the poet treats Sibyl's refusal to walk on the Holy Rood, which contains details from several different sources:

> Quen Þat scho to Þe cite cam,
> Scho cam in at Þat ilk ʒate,
> Þar Þis tre lay in hir gate,   8960
> Doun sho bowid hir to Þe grund,
> Þe tre scho honurd Þar a stound.
> Scho left hir syrte widuten schorne,
> And barfot wald ouer Þat borne,   8964
> And to Þat tre scho gan hir falde,
> And proohesy par-of scho tald;
> And namlyest of domes-day,
> Hou all Þis world suld wit of way. (87)   8968

After discussing many things with the Sibyl, Solomon gave her gifts and she returned to her home country. The poet concluded this section of his narrative of the Holy Rood by saying that it lay many a day ready in the temple until the time of Christ's passion:

> Þer it lay ful mani a day,
> Bot it was in Þe temple boun,
> At Þe time of cristes passion. (88)

In the "Cursor Mundi" version of the later episodes of the Holy Rood legend, the order of the incidents departs from that of Peter Comestor's "Histoia Scholastica". Even so, the spirit and the excitement surrounding the wonderful tree is maintained. The unknown poet of this religious poem has made a skillful compilation of episodes drawn from many sources. His treatment of this legendary material is bold, and he develops an elaborate tale that catches the interest of his reader. Though the material is apocryphal, he harmonizes it to be in keeping with his selections from the Old Testament, such as Moses, David and Solomon, and the central point of Christian history, the redemptive sacrifice of Christ on the Cross. The Jewish elements of the quest of Seth and the Christian elements of the legend of the Holy Rood are fused by the "Cursor" poet's creative imagination until they become one. His handling of the Myth of the Cross adds to the stated purpose of the "Cursor Mundi", that is, the education of the faithful Christian in the mysteries of his religion.

Further, the skillful use of these myths serve to heighten the climax of the "Cursor Mundi", as we shall examine in the following chapters in Christ's crucifixion and the Harrowing of Hell.

Chapter V
Climax in the Crucifixion

    In the two preceding chapters we have seen that prophecy and the myths of Seth and the Oil of Mercy, and of the Holy Cross have been used by the "Cursor" poet to bind together his narrative of salvation history. All the events described in the first fifteen thousand lines of this religious epic point forward to the greatest episode in human history – the Passion and death of Jesus Christ. This is the pivotal point of human history. To Medieval Man, whose life was theocentric, this was a simple fact. He thought of himself as living in the age of grace that followed Christ's death, and he expected the Second Coming to be an almost immediate event.

    In the twelfth century, the characteristic representation of the Crucifixion showed Christ in majesty, ruling from the cross. The cross, whose antecedent history we have followed through the Old Testament, functioned as a kind of earthly throne, rather than as the instrument of Christ's death. In the thirteenth century, however, this image changed greatly, in response to new meditational modes, new theological ideas, new fashions in sensibility: Christ the Savour is depicted suffering on the cross, his body broken and bleeding. (1) This transformation of Christianity's central image affected all art forms, including poetry. This can be seen best in the English Mystery cycles; they show Christ "don on Þe rood" in greater circumstantial detail, and with greater force and artistic complexity, than any other art from of the Middle Ages. (2)

The Narrative Unity of the Cursor Mundi

The treatment of the Crucifixion in the "Cursor Mundi" is similar to that found in other religious poems of this period, such as the "Northern Passion", the "South English Legendary", and the "Stanzaic Life of Christ". In these works the mood is grave and decorous, quite unlike that of the mature vernacular drama that developed late in the fourteenth century. The above Middle English poems have charm as well as several moving passages. The "Northern Passion", for instance, tells us,

> Ihesus suffered with gud will
> All payns þat þai wald putt him tyll,
> And so þau fore with him þat night
> Un-yo þat it was day full light,
> And þan þai said he sold be dede.

A couple of times during the crucifixion episode, the "Cursor" poet includes with personal observations powerful descriptive passages of the indignities and suffering Christ had to undergo. This is how he narrates the crowning with thorns:

A crune apon his heued þai sett	
of scharp tre was wroght,	
Þat in a hundred stedes, i-wiss,	16616
Þe in a hundred stedes, i-wiss,	
Þe red blod vte broght.	
[Þ]ai cled him in a mantil rede,	
toke of his auen wede,	16620
And siþen in his hand þau sett	
a mekil staf of rede;	
And wid him plaid sittisott,	
16624	16624
and bad þat he suld rede	
Quilk of þaim him gaue þe dint;	
sare agh þai for him drede.	
Sare þai agh þaim drede,	16628

> Þe folk Þat wat sua felle, (4)   16628

The poet then makes a personal interjection:

> Þe schame Þai on vr lauerd sought,
> ful store it war to telle! (5)

Later on after Christ has been nailed to the Cross, raised so all can see Him, the crowd mocks Him:

> Mekil heÞing Þai of him made,
> Bath sarazin and Iu, (6)

The poet declares that he cannot tell the tenth part of the crowd's spite:

> Te teind part of Þair despiitt,
> i mai noght tell to 3u!   16716

    The reason for the "Cursor Mundi" detailed attention given to both the crucifixion and events immediately leading up to it was a desire to make Christ's last hours on earth as vivid as possible, and prepare us for his glorious conquest of Hell, which will be dealt with in the next chapter. The emphasis is placed on those details, many of them legendary in origin that would appeal to clerics and laymen alike. The well-known events of Christ's passion are refashioned into an absorbing story, demanding from the hearers or readers the same human reactions as any of the popular contemporary romance: tears at the suffering of Our Lord, anger at the wickedness of the Jews, and later on triumph at Christ's Harrowing of Hell and Resurrection. Legends of unknown origin are grafted on to the account of the crucifixion that we find in four Gospels.

    One such legend for which H.C.W. Haenisch could find no source (8) concerns the cock that crew thrice after Peter's third denial of Christ to Judas. The poet inserts it after Peter comes face to face with Our Lord, and turns away weeping:

> [I]t es writen of Þis iudas
> quen he had done Þat sin,
> wid his penis Þat he tock,
> went till he moder in. (9)   15964

Judas tells his mother about his betrayal of Christ; she foretells his ruin, Christ's death and resurrection:

> "[S]un, has Þu Þi maistir sald?"
> "modir," he said, 'ȝa.'
> "Þu," scho said, "nu sal be scheint,
> i wat Þai will him sla,
> To dede Þu sal se him be done,   15980
> bot he sal rise Þer fra." (10)

Judas incredulously replies that Christ, once dead, can no more rise than yonder boiled cock. In the same moment the cock flies up and crows, and this crowing is the same that Peter heard. This is a dramatic scene between Judas and his mother. This is how the poet describes the miracle:

> "Rise vp modir eft? he said,
> "na sertis! ne bes it noght sua,
> [N]e sal he neuer rise eft,   15984
> treuli nou i Þe hight,
> Are sal Þis ilk coke vp rise
> was skaldid ȝisternight!"
> vnethes had he said Þe word,   15988
> Þe coke lep up on flight
> FeÞerid fairer Þan biforn,
> creu thoru grace of dright;
> And Þan bigan Þe traitor fals   15992
> to drede him for his pligh[t].

>[Þ]is it was Þat ilke coke,
>Þat petir herd him crau,
>Quen he ahd nitt his lauerd thrijs   15996
>he did him-seluen knau. (11)

This brief incident, like many similar ones, helps in tightening the whole frame of the "Cursor Mundi" by linking various events closer. The prophecy of Judas' mother is just one more of Christ's glorious resurrection. Nevertheless, the "Cursor" poet uses only a few of the legends that were current during the Medieval period. He ignores the grim story of three nails used in the crucifixion. The legend of the Forging of the Nails is found in the "Northern Passion". (12) It tells of the Jews going to a smith in the town to have the nails made. The smith who believed that Christ was a prophet, refused, saying that he had burned his hand and by a miracle it looked sore, though it really did not hurt him. The smith's wicked wife offered to make the nails, and with the Jews' help she made three rude nails:

>Þai war full great and rudely wroght
>Bot Þar fore Þai for soke Þam noght. (13)

The "Cursor" poet used good taste in his selection of stories to be included in his work. He does not make a random choice, but includes legends that assist in giving structural unity to his poem. He used good judgement in omitting the legend of the three nails, which is too anti-feminist for inclusion in the "Cursor Mundi", which is dedicated to the honour of Our Lady. Though it is an interesting story, it does not have links with other sections of the Passion as the legend of Peter's 'fair feathered' cock.

The "Cursor" poet has created his own "Harmony of the Gospels", (14) interweaving a continuous narrative based on the four evangelists' account of Christ's passion. It is enriched by the inclusion of legendary material which adds to the interest of the canonical description of the Christ's death. For instance, the "Cursor" poet takes the basic facts of Judas' death from Matthew and The Acts of the Apostles, (15) but adds colourful details to the episode. Judas procured a strong rope and hanged himself; his body burst; his soul went out through his belly because it might not come out at the mouth, which had kissed Christ:

> A rape he gat him preuili,
> Þat he wist was strang,
> And fast he fest aboute his hals,
> him-self Þar-wid he hang.   16504
> [v]te at his wamb Þe saule brast,
> at muth had it na wai,
> Þat he wid kist cristes muth,
> Als 3e are herd me say,   16508
> Quen he come als a traitor fals
> his auen lauerd to be-trai; (16)

The Medieval audience was interested in why Judas' body burst. The poet gives a satisfactory answer. No source has been found for this explanation of how Judas committed suicide by hanging himself.

    As we noted in the last chapter, the legend of the Holy Cross was one of the main threads binding the Old Testament section of the "Cursor Mundi" to the death of Christ: for on the "tree of life" he was crucified.

    After Christ had been condemned, the Jews looked about for wood to make his Cross. They went to the temple and cut the King's tree and found it was still fresh and sound. (17) This they took for the Cross:

> [I]esus crist, vr sauueur,
> was dampned to do of dau,   16544
> To be hanged on a tre,
> als Þan was thefis lau.

> Bot swilk a tre þaim wanted alle
> als writen es in sau; 16548
> Þai said þai wold þe kinges tre
> Vnto þat mister sau,
> For it was commanded þai it suld
> vte of þe temple suith, 16552
> in tua þis tre þai schare,
> Als mekil als þai sau þat gained,
> Þai tok þaim and na mare.
> Þai fand it als nu and fress 16556
> als it on stouid ware.

Thus the wood from the three pippin seeds given to Seth when he went to the gates of Paradise to ask for the Oil of Mercy for his aged father is used to make Christ's cross. This shows the artistic achievement of unity in the "Cursor Mundi". The poet has succeeded in the remarkable feat of weaving the Oil of Mercy of the Holy Rood myths through sixteen thousand lines of verse, telling of the important events of Scriptural history. The importance of relating the fall of Adam to the redemption of mankind by Christ on the cross is one of the prime objectives of this work.

The poet continues his descriptions of the making of the cross by remarking that even though the tree could easily be shaped and cut the men could not stir it a foot. Caiphas sent two hundred men to fetch it, but in vain. Thus the tree continued to show its strange powers. When it was finished, Christ was brought. He bowed down to the cross and kissed it. It miraculously rose onto His back without help and He carried it forth. There is no known source for this miracle, which is related thus in the "Cursor Mundi":

> Quen it was wroght þai all ne moght
> stir it vte of þe stede,
> Bituix and þat ur lauerd crist
> was þedir him-seluen ledd. 16584

> [Q]uen he come to þat suete tre
> þe felunes to him said,
> "Take it vp," þai said, "þu seis
> hu it es to þe graid.:
> hu it es to þe graid." 16588
> He lutede dune and kist it sone,
> and at þe first braid,
> Widvten ani help of man
> Vpon his bac it laid. 16592
> [I]nto þe tune forth he it bare,
> bifor þat cursed lede. (19)

It is at this stage in the passion narrative that the whole legend of the cross from the quest of Seth to the martyring of Maximilla is inserted in the Oxford Manuscript of the "Northern Passion". (20) The "Cursor" poet shows greater artistic skill in spacing his account of the legend as we have seen, through the first nine thousand lines of his work,

The measurements of the cross are given as four-and-one-half ells long and half an ell broad,

> Half feird ellen was þe lenth,
> and oþer hald þe brede, (21) 16600

The legend mentioned before has other numbers,

> Viii cubits þai made it lang
> With outen þat in þe erth suld gang, 792
> And aþer side of cubits thre
> þat abouen þe heuid suld be; (22)

Simon the Cyrenian, (23) who is pressed into carrying Christ's cross to Calvary, is not mentioned by name. He is merely referred to as a "bisen man", which can mean either a busy man or a workman. It was not the Roman custom to make the condemned carry the whole cross to the place of crucifixion. The cross-beam (patibulum) was borne by the criminal to the place of execution, while his "titulus" or tablet of accusation was hung round his neck, or carried before his by a herald. Christ's "title" was written by "Sir Pilate" in Hebrew, Greek and Latin. It was placed over his head on the cross:

> [A]bourn his heued, als i ȝu tell,
> a bord was festind plat, 11684
> Þar-on it was þe titel writen,
> thoru rede of sir pilat.
> "Iesus nazarene, of iuus king,"
> Þar apon he wrat, 11688
> Of ebru, gru, and latine,
> for to schind his state. (24)

It is noteworthy that in a poem as long as the "Cursor Mundi", the poet devotes only ten lines to a description of the actual crucifixion and the raising of the cross. This is in contrast to the "Northern Passion", which takes fifty-eight lines of verse to describe the putting of Christ on the cross, while in the York play the dialogue accompanying the action of nailing Christ to the cross amount to more than two hundred and fifty lines of text. One can read a convincing description of a crucifixion, as we have in this work, much quicker than it can be acted out on the stage. The "Cursor" poet does not dwell on his account of the nailing of Christ to the cross. The brevity of his narrative of this incident adds to the horror and wanton cruelty of the action. The Roman soldiers who carried out Pontius Pilate's orders are referred to as "Knights" by the "Cursor" poet. (25) This is in keeping with the work's medieval fashion of making narratives contemporary in tone. This is how the crucifying of Our Lord is told in this poem:

> [Þ]e knightes þat war wid him sett, 16664
> Þai iesu sone un-ciede,

> And led him to þat rode tre
> and led him to þar rode tre,
> and þar-on þai him sprede,   16668
> þar he gaue his suete flesse
> ????? ransun in wede,
> ????? haue merci on vs,
> þat sua sare for vs blede!   16672
> [Þ]ai nailed him opon þat tre,
> on þe monet caluare,
> And a thef on eþer side
> þai hinged þar him bi,   16676
> þat þai all suld vndersatnd
> ȝode þat wai bi,
> Of þir tua theues, als qua sai,
> "þair maistir thef am I."   16680

The insertion of a prayer in the middle of a descriptive passage is quite oftem found in the "Cursor Mundi". Here we have a brief, concise telling of the actia; nailing of Christ to the cross. Christ's only reply to the indignities and tortures he has undergone is:

> "Fadir," he said, "forgiue þu þaim
> þat þai do gaines me,   16696
> For quat þai do þai er sua blind,
> þai can nought seluen se." (27)

Thus the poet gives emotional intensity to Christ's: "They know not what they do." (28) The "Cursor'poet, however, adds to St. Luke, "They are so blind, they cannot see themselves." Christ was killed by those he loved ad came to save –by those He loved, not by those He hated. This is the one of the great paradoxes of the crucifixion. The "Stanzaic Life of Christ" discussed it in this way:

> For law wonder had ben i-wys
> Yif he of enmys suffird hade

> To guych he done hade er amys,
> sich manas the e he hade made,
> Or of alien and stranger
> that had no knowen him befire,
> but of his frendes and verray feres
> He tholet that grevet mich þe more. (29)

The men who should be His friend, though they scorn Him and kill Him, are not aware of what they really do. This fact, central to the mystery of the Passion, is kept in mind by the "Cursor" poet in his handling of the crucifixtion. He focuses his attention soley on Christ, and the great live He had for all men, even those who were appointed as His executioners. The poet sought to reveal as much as he could of the pathos and dignity of His suffering. Nothing is allowed to take our interest away from Christ during the episode, not like the "japing" and "jesting" of the "tortures" in the medieval drama that overshadows Christ and his suffering on the stage.

The "Cursor" poet continues his narration of the crucifixion with the telling of the story of the penitent thief. The "Cursor Mundi" calls the two criminals crucified with Christ, Dismis and Gesmas. (30) The poet may have taken them from the "Gospel of Nicodemus", (31) which he used for a later section, or he may have learnt them from some other source, considering the general acquaintance with these legends in the Middle Ages. Gesmas joins the passers-by in upbraiding Christ, while the other, Dismas, says they deserved their doom, but Christ is blameless. He goes on to ask Our Lord for mercy. The details are taken chiefly from Luke, who is the only evangelist to mention the two robbers. The poet expands Dismas' rebuke:

"Þu dreded litil god,
Þat þis paine es on laid.   16724
[L]ittil dredis þu drightin,
or his mekil might,
Þe dome þat es nu giuen on vs,

> We haue it all wid tight; 16728
> And Þis man, wat we wele Þat he
> Es all widvten plight.
> Haue merci lauerd! On me quen Þu bes
> In Þi rike sua bright! " (32) 16732
> Christ replies:
> "forsoth to Þe i hight,
> Þat Þu sal be in paradis
> wid me Þis ilke night." (33) 16736

Echoes of the legend of the Good Theif are met with here, that the poet may have expected his audience to know. On the supposition that Our Lord was crucified upon March 25, the Roman Martyrology for this day contains the following entry: "At Jerusalem the commemoration of the holy thief who confessed Christ upon the cross and deserved to hear from Him the words: 'This day shalt thou be with me in paradise.'" In the Arabic "Gospel of the Infancy" we are told how, in the course of the flight into Egypt, robbers assailed the Holy Family. Of the two leaders, one was stirred by compassion, besought his companion to let them pass unmolested, and when he refused, bribed him with forty drachmas, so that the Virgin Mary and St. Joseph were left in peace. Thereupon Mary said to her benefactor, "The Lord God shall sustain thee with his right hand and give thee remission of sins" And the Infant Jesus, intervening, spoke, "And after thirty years, mother, the Jews will crucify me in Jerusalem, and these two robbers will be lifted on the cross with me." (34) This legendary story, with others, subsequently found popular acceptance in western Christendom during the Middle Ages, though the names of the robbers vary, the most commonly given were Dismas and Gestas. We find the two thieves represented in pictures of the crucifixion during the medieval period. Although the poet was acquainted with a version of the Gospels of Christ's Infancy, he most likely did not know the Arabic version in which this story is narrated.

The "Cursor" poet does not dwell on Christ's last agonies.

After mentioning the names of the four who "stode bi Þe rode tre" – His mother, Mary Magdalene, Mary Cleophas and His favorite disciple, John – he gives Christ's seven words from the Cross:

> "Modir, iohn sal be Þi sun
> fra nu, instead of me,   16760
> And Þi modir dere cosin,
> Þu loke hir hir," said je, (35)

The poet then describes how the light dimmed about the ninth hour, and other wonderful phenomena. The climax of the poem is soon reached; Christ cries out:

> "To Þe fadir ӡeilde i mi gast,
> nu haue i done Þi will.: (36)

And dies.

In normal Roman crucifixion the pains of death were protracted, sometimes for days. Even when the victims were nailed and not merely tied to the cross, it was hunger and exhaustion, not loss of blood, that was the direct cause of death. Sometimes an end was put to their sufferings by the breaking of the crucified victim's legs by hammer strokes. In the case of Christ, however, His suffering on the cross lasted three hours only due in part to the tortures He had previously undergone. Pontius Pilate gave orders that the crucified men were to be put to death because the following day was not only a Sabbath, but the Sabbath of Passover week. This is how the poet explains it:

> [Þ]e iuus for Þe mekil fest,
> Þat on Þe moru suld be,   16824
> Þai said Þat bodi suld be nane
> Left hangand on Þe tre, (37)

The soldier broke the thighs of the two thieves who were found still alive;

> Þe tua Þai fand sumdel in lijf,
> Of eÞer Þai brac Þe thie. (38)

Turning to Christ, they found he had already expired:

> [B]ot quen Þat Þai till iesus come,
> Þai fand him dede as stone,   16832
> For Þai wist Þat he was dede,
> Of him Þai brac no bone. (39)

The "Cursor" poet then narrates how Longinus, the "blind knight", ran his spear into Christ's side. Blood and water gushed out. (40) A drop of the precious blood spurting from the wound falls on the blind soldier's eye and his sight is restored. There is a considerable literature connected with the legend of Longinus and the Holy Lance. The "centurian" of Mark (XV, 29) is often identified with the "soldier" of John (XIX, 34) who pierced the side of Christ, and both are connected with Longinus who is first named in the "Acts of Pilate" portion of the "Gospel of Nicodemus." The "Cursor" poet would have come acros the apocryphal tale either in the "Gospel of Nicodemus" of the "Legenda aurea". (41) He tells the legend briefly:

> Bot longeus Þe blind, wid a spere
> (of knightes was he one)   16836
> Thorus his side vnrekenli
> apon his herte it rane;
> [B]lod and water vte of his side ran,
> seleuth mekil wane,   16840
> And of Þat blod ran till hijs ei
> he gate jis sight on-ane

The poet gives his authority for this miracle as Saint John:

> He Þat sau it Þus he said,
> his witness es, saint iahne,
> For Þat man of his freinschip,
> was sua ner was bi him ane. 16848

Another legend, for which no source has been found, has it that the cross blossomed from midday until evening;

> Þ]e rode it was wid lieif and brac
> florist wele selcuthli, 16860
> Fra Þe middai to Þe complene
> Þat mani toght farli ;
> Bot Þogh Þe iuus Þat it sau
> thoght seleuth ne for-Þi, 16864
> NouÞer Þai gaue man, ne Þai toke
> Ensample god Þar-bi;
> Bot on Þe morn of Þat greening,
> Þe tre als ar was dri. 16868

The poet then describes the descent from the cross, remarking with regard to Our Lady:

> [Þ]e murning Þat his moÞer made
> mai a man rede in rune. (45) 16880

Joseph of Arimeathiae, who had begged Christ's body of Pontius Pilate, attempted to get possession of the Holy rood. The Jews, however, prevented him, and secretly buried it that same night. Again, we have no known source for this episode, which helps connect the crucifixion with the finding of the cross by Saint Helen, which we will examine in chapter VII. This is how the "Cursor" poet handles this brief linking section:

> [I]oseph wald haue a-wai Þe rode,
> Þe iuus him forbedd,

> Þat ilke night Þaim-self it did
> a-way for to be ledd;   16916
> wid Þe theifs croices tuin,
> quen all war gane to bed,
> And groue Þaim thre for cristen men,
> widin a preue stedd.   16920
> of him Þat Þar-on bledd. (46)

The portion of the "Cursor Mundi" on the crucifixion closes with the reflections of the poet. He meditates on the fact that Christ is buried and now all hopes of holy church hang on Our Blessed Lady. Thus the poet returns to the Virgin Mary, in whose honor he has undertaken the task of writing his poem. The "Cursor poet declares:

> [N]u es Þe crois grauen vnder grete,
> and iesus vnder stane,
> And hinges all hope of hali kire   16924
> in mari mild allane.
> Ay til iesus Þe third dai
> had fughten again sathane, (47)

The poet then reminds us that mankind was made slaves through a tree, and now was liberated through one;

> [T]hour a tre, als ȝe haue herd,
> was all man-kind mad thrall,
> And throru his hali rode tre,
> Þan war we frelsed all.   16942
> Again Þat appil adam ete
> was giuen iesus Þe gall, (48)

It is the history of the pippen seeds that became the Holy Rood that has been the material that had bound tightly the tale of our salvation in the hand of the skilfil "Cursor" poet. He has told its history in a style resembling that of the chivalric romances.

The seventeen hundred odd lines that are devoted to Christ's passion and death are in balance with the rest of the long poem. The gospel account of these events is supplemented by several legends, some dealing with the cross. The immediate source of a number of these is unknown and may have been invented by the "Cursor" poet himself. The sadness of the events described is expressed in moving poetry. We are left with the mourning Virgin Mary, while Christ descends into Hell. In the next chapter, we deal with the Harrowing of Hell, which for Medieval man was one of the most popular episodes in the whole of religious history. This is the second climax of the "Cursor Mundi". It is here that Adam finally received the Oil of Mercy, which is Christ Himself.

Chapter VI
The Harrowing of Hell

    Perhaps the "Cursor" poet's greatest skill as a story-teller is seen in his handling of the popular Medieval episode surrounding Christ's Harrowing of Hell. For in this section of the poem, he makes use of the flashback technique as well as prophecy. He thus gathers together here all the threads of the past and the future, and shows the triumphant Christ, who was Himself the long awaited Oil (1) of Mercy, promised to Adam when he was expelled from the Garden of Eden.

    The ultimate source of this portion of the "Cursor Mundi" is to be found in the early Christian Apocryphal "Gospel of Nicodemus" (2) itself an appendix to a book called "Acts of Pilate". (3) There are versions of this work in Greek, Coptic, and Latin; and translation of them could have been available to the "Cursor" poet. The version that M.R. James calls Latin A is behind the typical English Medieval renderings of myth. (4)

    The story of the "Gospel of Nicodemus" is that, after Christ had died on the cross and before His Resurrectionm Adam and Eve and other souls who were living in the darkness of Hell suddenly felt the warmth of the sun and saw the shining of a bright light. Whereupon Adam and the other patriarchs and John the Baptist rejoiced and began talking hopefully among themselves. Seth then recalled how, when his father Adam lay sick, he went to the gates of Paradise and begged the archangel Michael for the Oil of Mercy with which to heal his father's body. Michael could not give it to him, but added the Son of God would give it after several thousand years had elapsed. All the patriarchs rejoiced at Seth's word, knowing that the deliverance was near. There follows an agitated dialogue between Satan and Hell, for they know that some disaster threatens them. They were particularly agitated because it was but recently that they were deprived of Lazarus. As they are talking, there is heard a cry calling for the gates of Hell to open so that the King of Glory may enter. Satan and Hell determine to bar the gates still more strongly. The patriarchs renew the cry to open the gates. The next cry is a climax and decides the issue; and here is how the Apocryphal Gospel continues:

> And there came a great voice as of thunder saying: Remove, O prince, your gates, and be ye lift up, ye everlasting doors, and the King of Glory shall come in. And when Hell saw that they so cried out twice, he said, as if he knew it not: Who is the King of Glory? And David answered Hell and said: The Lord strong and mighty, the Lord Mighty in battle, He is the King of Glory…And now, O thou most foul and stinking Hell, open thy gates that the King of Glory may come in. And as David spake thus unto Hell, the Lord of Majesty appeared in the form of a man and lightened the eternal darkness and brake the bonds that could not be loosed; and the succor of His everlasting might visited us that sat in the deep darkness of our transgressions and in the shadow of death of our sins. (5)

The powers of Hell then expressed their terror and quarreled among themselves, while Christ, taking Adam by the right hand, gathers his saints around Him and makes the Sign of the Cross over them, and still holding Adam by the hand, "went up and out of Hell, and all the saints followed Him." Finally, he delivered them all to the archangel Michael to be housed in Paradise. Enouch, Elias, and the penitent thief join them on their way there.

The substance of the "Gospel of Nicodemus" is as early

as the second century, though the developed Gospel itself may be two centuries later; and by the age of Constantine its central event, the releasing of Adam from Hell by Christ, and become a subject for the artists. After the turn of the millennium it became excessively common, both in the Byzantine and the western artistic traditions. The church ceremony beginning "Exultet jam angelica turba caelorum" took place on Easter Eve and includes a reference to the descent into Hell. The so-called "Exultet Rolls" from South Italy, dating from the tenth to the twelfth centuries, gives illustrations of the different parts of the ceremony. (6)

Though there is an Old English version of the "Gosoel of Nicodemus" (7), the theme of the Harrowing of Hell became more fully developed in the thirteenth century Britain. Once this had happened, the literature of the late Middle Ages in England reposed on the authority and security of the great myth and was content to reproduce it unpretentiously and loyally. Only exceptionally did it add to the myth or seek to fashion it anew. On the other hand the literature is less uniform in treatment than is the art. For the artist the dramatic moment was when Christ, having burst the gates of Hell, took Adam by the hand; and he always chose that movement, however much else he succeeded in implying. In the literature the rescue of Adam is nearly always paramount, and the "Cursor Mundi" is no exception.

The "Cursor" poet's treatment of the Harrowing of Hell, coming after he had written more than seventeen thousand lines, shows no relaxation of vitality. He versifies the whole of the myth as found in the "Gospel of Nicodemus" and adds touches of his own. For example, John the Baptist is not just there is Hell along with the rest but appears there after the light has shone in. Seth does not merely tell his story of the oil of Paradise but is asked by Adam to tell it. Further the author seems to have taken the pictures of the myth very much to heart, for he makes Christ take Adam by the hand no less than three times.

The "Cursor" poet acknowledges his debt to the "Gospel of Nicodemus" directly:

> Þarfor wrought nichodeme a writ,
> I tell nu wid Þi leue of it.   17288

The poet appears to have used one of the now missing early Middle English versions of the Harrowing of Hell, (9) which follows closely the Apocryphal work. He begins this section of his poem with a free translation of the twelfth chapter of the "Gospel of Nicodemus". The following lines of the "Cursor Mundi", which will be followed by the Latin text translated by M.R. James, may suffice to show the poet's method:

> [O]f ioseph, quen Þe iuus wist
> Þat he had doluen iesu crist,
> Þai wid him ful wrath & wod,
> And all formenged in Þaur mod.   17292
> Þai sent Þair sergantz forto nim
> Bath sir nichodeme and him;
> And oÞer twelue Þat for him space
> Quen Þat Þai soght iesu wid sake,   17296
> Al Þai hidd Þaim-self to ʒeme,
> Bot fort Þan come sir nichodeme.
> For he was ouer Þe iuus Þan,
> Als Þair prins and ouer-man.   17300
> He come to Þaim in Þat siquar,
> Þat in Þair sinagog Þai war,
> He said "ʒe men, murtherers sua curs,
> Hu dar ʒe cum in goddess hus!"   17304
> Þai said, "bot quat Þar-in dos Þu?
> Þat sua spac and held wid iesu.
> Þi part mot euer and wid him be."
> "Amen, amen, amen," said he   17308

Let us compare this passage with the opening of chaper twelve of the "Gospel of Nicodemus":

> Now when the Jew heard that Joseph had begged the body of Jesus, they sought for him and for the twelve men which said that Jesus was not born of fornication, and for Nicodemus and many others which had come forth before Pilate and declared his good works. But all they hid themselves, and Nicodemus only was seen of them, for he was a ruler of the Jews. And Nicodemus said unto them: Hoe came ye into the synagogue? The Jews say unto him: How didn't thou come into the synagogue? For thou art confederate with him, and his portion shall be with in the life to come. Nicodemus saith: Amen. Amen. Amen. (11)

The "Cursor Mundi" passage is quite a close translation of the Apocryphal Scripture. The next two hundred and seventy lines of the "Cursor Mundi" (12) is a close paraphrase of chapters twelve to fifteen of the Latin "Gospel of Nicodemus."

Earlier, at line 17575, the author makes a digression on the blindness of the Jews of Our Lord's day. This pause is the narrative enables the poet to comment on the action – a technique found throughout the work. (13) The poet declares:

> Walawai! quat Þa men war blind,
> Quen Þai went sua iesus to find.   17576
> For him to find qua wille him seke,
> Þair mode till him Þam most Þai meke,
> To knau him drightin all weildand,
> Þan man Þai find him bune at hand,   17580
> Mightili in all his need,
> To suilk he wille his bodi bede.
> For Þoght he sitt in heuenes hall,
> ȝeit he is in erd ouer alle,   17584
> Mightili bath fer and nere,

>And nouÞer mist in heuen ne here.
>Þai Þat traistli in him trous,
>His bliscing to Þa men buus; (14)   17688

Then the poet returns to the "Gospel of Nicodemus" to narrate how the Jews seek for the risen Christ in vain, and how Nicodemus finds Joseph of Arimathiae, who had been miraculously delivered from prison. Joseph relates to the Jewish leaders how Christ came to him, blessed him and led him to the tomb, where he showed him to his own house in Arimathiae, bidding him to remain there for the next forty days. The Jews are struck with terror and confounded by Joseph's tale.

With the story of the resurrection of Simeon's two sons from Hell the poet commences to deal with the Harrowing of Hell proper at line 17781. The time is some forty days after Christ rose from the tomb. Two young men have also come back to life. They are the sons of Simeon, who took the infant Jesus in his arms when he was presented in the temple; they have come back to life at the moment when Christ rose from the dead. (15) Joseph of Arimathiae tells Anna and Caiaphas that Simeon's two sons, who were buried in Arimathiae, rose with Christ from the dead, and are now going around the town, kneeling and praying but speaking with no one. This is how the "Cursor" poet states it;

>Gas, seis nu, for Þe hali-dome,
>And 3e sal find Þair tumbes tume;
>In mi cite of arimathi,
>Þar er Þai walkand witterli.   17800
>Þar men seis Þaim in Þat tune,
>In kneling state and orisune;
>Ai vmquile men heris Þaim cri,
>Bot wid nane speke Þai of Þat bi. (16)   17804

Joseph makes the dramatic suggestion that these two brothers who have come back to life be found and questioned. He cries:

> Ga we Þan fulsumli Þeder,
> And fand we forto bring Þaim heder,
> And sal we Þaim wid coniuring,
> Ger tell vs of Þis vp-rising." (17)   17808

The Jewish leaders agree on this course of action. Anna and Caiaphas, accompanied by Nicodemus, Joseph of Arimathiae and others seek for Carius and Lenthius. The group also includes Gamaliel ("Of him es noght bot trenth to tell"). (18) The inclusion of Gamaliel, the distinguished Pharasee scholar, is found in chapter seventeen of the "Gospel of Nicodemus":

> And Anna and Caiaphas, Nicodemus and Joseph and Gamaliel went and found them not in their sepulcher, but they went unto the city of Arimathiae and found them there, kneeling on their knees and giving themselves unto prayer. (19)

All are keen to find out the truth and the two brothers are brought back to Jerusalem, and are conjured to tell honestly how they were raised to life. Both Carius and Lethius trembled and groaned, asked for parchment, and said they would write what they had heard and saw. Even though they sat separately, their accounts of their experiences beyond the grave were identical. This is a skillful way of obtaining an eyewitness account of the "secret works" of Christ during His descent into Hell.

This is a skillful way of obtaining an eye-witness account of the "secret works" of Christ during His descent into Hell. This is the great climax of this long religious poem. Here the myth of the Oil of Mercy and the legend of the Cross meet. The artistic unity of the "Cursor Mundi" is seen in the way the poet has developed and expanded his legendary material to this point when he pulls the various threads of the narrative together in the Harrowing of Hell as told by Simeon's sons. The poet says:

> [Q]uen carius and lenthius
> was coniured of Þir iuus Þus,
> wid all Þair fless Þai quoke onane,
> And wid Þair hertis gun Þai grame.   17836
> Till heuen Þai lifted Þair eien brad,
> And on Þair tunges Þe takni[n]g made
> wid Þair fingres all of Þe crois,
> And alsone spac wid manes vois.   17840
> "Lauerd," Þai said, (Þat hei dright-in
> Þan bad Þai giue Þaim parchemine)
> "We sal ȝu write and nathing lij
> Quat we herd and sau wid ei." (20)   17844

The fact that the account of Christ's descent into Hell is written down by two eye-witnesses whose accounts are similar, gives it the appearance of truth. The Carius and Lethius description of the Harrowing of Hell is some six hundred and four lines in length and is the pivotal point of the "Cursor Mundi". It tells how God gives Adam the long-promised Oil of Mercy. The account of Simeon's sons commences with a prayer:

> "[L]auerd iesu crist," said Þai,
> "Godd, Þat all Þir mightes may,
> Þat es upras of dede and lijf,
> And has vs kid Þe right sua rijf,   17868
> Þu late vs lauerd, wid leue of Þe,
> To tell nu of Þi auen priuite.
> Thoru dede of Þi suete croice
> For Þu bad we suld na man tell,   17864
> Þi dedis dern Þu did in hell, --
> Þe dedis of Þi maieste, --
> Bot thoru Þi-self coniurd er we,
> SiÞen it es sua nu most we need   17860
> Þe mightes tell of Þi god-hede. (21)

Thus our only knowledge of Christ's "dern deeds" come from the penned account by these two holy men. Carius and his brother write that while waiting in the mournful place, suddenly a golden light shone upon them.

> [A]ls we war satd in mu[rn]ful stall,
> we self and vr eldris all,   17872
> Brathli þar brast a golden leme,
> Brighter þan ani sunes beme,
> Sua right purprin heu es nane,
> Þis ilk light apon vs schene. (22)   17868

This light, which is brighter than any rays of sun, rouses the captive souls of Adam and his descendants who are awaiting the Oil of Mercy. Adam "that was man for most," and the patriarchs and prophets begin to rejoice as they sit on their dark seats. Adam fittingly is the first to speak:

> "Þis ilke lght forsoth es he
> Þat maker es of lastand light
> Nu has he sent vs þat he hight." (23)   17876

All realize that the salvation is at hand. Adam's declaration that the maker of eternal light has now sent what he had promised is followed by an announcement by Isaiah. Chapter eighteen of the "Gospel of Nicodemus" runs thus:

> And Isaiah cried out and said:
>> This is the light of the Father, even the Son of God, according as I prophesied when I lived upon the earth: The land of Zabulon and the land of Nephthalem beyond the Jordan, of Galiilee of the Gentiles, the people that walked in darkness have seen a great light, and they that dwell in the land of the shadow of death, upon them did the light

shine. And now hath it come and shone upon us that sit in death. (24)

In the corresponding passage of the "Cursor Mundi", the Holy prophet cries out:

> 'Þis light it es of goddess sun
> Þat i in erd tell of was won. 17880
> Þe folk in dedeli mirknes stadd
> Sau grete light Þat made Þaim glad,
> Þat light es nu apon vs schede
> Þar we sitte in Þe schadu of dede.' (25) 17884

There is little doubt that the "Cursor" poet used either the "Gospel of Nicodemus" or a paraphrase of it for this section of his monumental work.

Next to speak in this drama is none other than the father of Carius and Lethius, Simeon. This righteous and devout man had taken the infant Jesus in his arms when He was presented in the temple. (26) Simeon said:

> "ȝe thank drightin, nu cums i ȝu ro, 17888
> vr lauerd iesu crist Þe blisse,
> All-mighti god es fader hiss.
> In temple was he me bitaght,
> And ȝung in armis i him light; 17894
> Þe hali gast Þus did me mele,
> Mine eien lauerd has sene Þi hele,
> Þe quilk Þu has Þi folk fordight
> Of israel, wid blissful light." (27) 17898

On hearing this, all the saints in hell rejoice the more. The excitement mounts as a man who seems to have been a hermit approaches Adam and his companions. On being challenged, he replies that he is John the Baptist:

> ., 'i hate iohn,
> Iohn es mi nam, voice and prophete,
> Biddand forto graith þe street, 17904
> To graith þe wai for cristes face,
> Þat till his folk sal grant vs grace. (28)

John goes on to narrate how he baptized Christ in the river Jordan and heard a voice from heaven, saying "this is my son, my dear." He also warns the saints that Christ will soon visit them:

> Comen es i nu forwid þat king,
> Bodword of his cum to bring,
> Goddes sun sal ȝu sone visite, 17920
> He cums at hand to slak ȝur site.
> He þat es bred to slak ȝur site.
> He þat es bred sua hei of strand,
> Nu comes to se þis laithli land.' (29) 17924

When Old Adam heard that Christ, who had been baptized in the Jordan, was on his way to this loathsome country, he called Seth, as we have mentioned above, to tell about the Oil of Mercy. He charged his son thus:

> 'sun tell til vs all 17928
> Þe sothfastnes, and na thing hele,
> All þat þu herd of saint michaele
> Archangele, quen i þe gan wis
> To þe ȝatis of paradies, 17932
> To prai vr lauerd drightin dere,
> To send me wid his messagere
> Þe oyle of his merciful tre,
> Þat i, seke, moght smerled be.' (30) 17936

Seth tells us how he had gone to the gates of Paradise on the request of the aged Adam and had a conversation with Saint Michael. The archangel told him that it was no use toiling after the oil, for Adam must wait five thousand, one hundred years. Saint Michael told him:

> His auen sun sal he send dune
> In erde, Þat mani sal mistron,
> Þi fadir cors vp sal he rais,
> And als of oÞer in Þakin dais.   17960
> Þou halier Þan he be nane
> Houen sal he be in flom iordane.
> Quen he sal stei vp of Þat strand,
> Þat oyle he sal bring in his hand,   17964
> Of his merci to smerl all wid
> Þat sekes treuth wid his grace or right,
> And till all Þaa Þat bers Baptist
> To lastand lijf in name of crist.   17968
> Þat goddes sun sua, mekil of might,
> Þat mang mankin als man sal lght,
> Sal bring Þi fader adam and his
> Of hell to paradis of blis.' (31)   17972

Thus Christ Himself will bring the Oil of Mercy to anoint all the patriarchs and prophets who kept God's covenant. When those in hell heard Seth, they were filled with elation.

The "Cursor" poet with the aid of Apocryphal Gospels and legendary material, had made a strong connection between the Fall of Adam, the Quest of Seth and the Harrowing of Hell. In the early centuries of the Christian era, Christ was customarily shown as victorious on the cross. The crucifixion was understood as the great moment in salvation history. But by the time the "Cursor Mundi" was written in the beginning of the fourteenth century, the dying and the victory of Christ were conceived separately: the victory was postponed until Our Lord had harrowed hell. The traditional statement of His triumph there was thought of as a struggle or knightly combat in which he jousts with Satan for the soulds of the Just who died prior to this. A fourteenth century sermon extant in three English manuscripts describes the armour worn by Christ in his encounter with Satan in the underworld and includes this detail:

> "Pro equo habuit crucem super quam pependit; prosento apposuit latus suum, et processit sic contra inimicum cum lancea, non in mana sed stykand in his side." (32)

As a prologue to the struggle between Christ and Satan for man's soul, the "Cursor" poet gives a discussion between Satan, the duke of death, with Hell. Both become agitated at the joyful cries of the saints when Seth finished his story. There follows a strange dialogue between Satan and Hell. The former tells the latter to make ready to receive Christ, who while on earth claimed to be God's son. He complains:

> Þat i made wode, halt, blind, and mesel
> wid word allane he gaue þaim hele,   17996
> I taght þe dede men als þin auen,
> Bot quilk he has þaim fra þe drauen." (33)

Hell is perturbed and wonders who Christ really is, fearing the deliverance of his prisoners from death. He asks Satan:

> Quat es he?
> Quatkin a man es þat iesis?   18000
> Þat werrsos on þe euer-ai quare,
> And siþen es dredand dede sua sare.
> Siþen his manhed es suilk of might,
> Qua mau þan gain his goddehed fight?   18004
> O sai, siþen he es all weilldand,
> Es na thing mai his will widstand.
> Qui dredes he dede? Þu wate noght, na,

> Noght bot forto suike Þe sua   18008
> He will Þe take and waif in wa
> To lend Þar-in euer and a.'

Satan is scornful of Hell's prophecy, saying that he made the Jewish elders rise against Christ, and that death will now bring him here. Hell is not convinced. He reminds Satan that Christ was the same person who drew the dead away from him. Others by prayer have stolen the dead, but Christ does it by His word. He concludes by warning:

> Mai fall Þis es Þat ilk iesus,
> Þat stinkand lazarun fra vs   18040
> Of his erding Þe thridd dai
> He losed him, and led away,
> Þe quilk al dede him quick he ʒald,
> His word widstand had i no wald.' (35)   18044

Satan admits that Christ has vexed them in many ways. Then Hell forbids Satan to bring Christ there because he realizes that He is God. Thus even the powers of darkness finally are forced to acknowledge who Christ really is –

> wele wat i nu, and wenis noght,
> Þat he Þat suilkin mightes moght   18064
> Ed godd stalworth weildand in will
> And manhed mighti forto fulfill,
> And es sauueor of manes lede,
> All Þat her here spred wid me   18068
> In presun of mu creuelte,
> Dune in dome of dede sua dim,
> To lijf he sal Þaim lede wid him.' (36)

The mystery cycles which are of a later date than the "Cursor Mundi" (37) also have a dialogue in hell between Satan and his devils. But here Satan in not all powerful, Hell appears to be his equal. He has doubts on his own and Satan's powers to hold Jesus Christ.

It is at this dramatic point in Simeon's sons' narration of the Harrowing of Hell that a loud clear ghostly voice cries:

> ȝe princes of helle, vndoes ȝur ȝate!
> Þe king of blis will haue in-late.' (38)

This command of Christ electrifies Hell who turns on Satan. He casts him out of the underworld, crying:

> "Þu do Þe neÞen fra me, sathan!   18080
> A faint fighter me thin cert Þu,
> Hu sal Þu fight again iesu?"

Then he shuts his brazen gates with bars of steel, hoping to keep Christ outside.

> 'Bot opin vp Þin ȝates wide,
> Lat in Þe king, widvten bide!   18084
> In sal he c[u]me, Þe king of blis." (40)

Both King David and Isaiah proclaim to the waiting throng of saints that this is indeed the long-awaited Messiah. While they speak, the gates of hell are forced open –

> Þan brast Þe brasen ȝate sua strang,
> And stelin lock Þat Þar-on hang. (41)

Christ again in a voice that sounds like thunder from heaven, commands that the gates be opened wide for the King of bliss. David replies that he knows well that voice:

> 'For i wid prophecy had hight

> Thoru Þe haligastes might,   18136
> And Þat i tald of forwid Þan
> I sai ȝu nu, wele i it can.
> Þe lauerd Þat es sua mekil of might,
> Þat es sua strang and stif in light,   18140
> Þe blissful king Þis es Þat ilke,
> For Þar mai be nanoÞer suilk.
> He Þat beheld fra heuen doune
> To here Þe plant of his presume,   18144
> Of his sinful sighand sua sare,
> To lese Þaim vte of band of care.
> And Þu hell, sua fule stinand sting,
> vndo, lare in Þe blissful king!' (42)   18148

No sooner had David finished his speech than Christ enters hell. The light that radiated from Him broke all fetters and bands of sorrow of the throng and dispersed the shadows. At this point, the "Cursor" poet lets Carius and Lethius describe the results of Our Lord's entrance into hell,

> Þz waful wras sua dedeli dim,
> All lighted Þe leme Þat come wid him,   18156
> Brast all Þe bandes of vr site,
> And visited vs wid grete delite,
> In Þat mirknes Þar we lay,
> Euer in night widuten day. (43)   18160

They say that "the bands of their sorrow" were burst by the ray of shining light of coming Christ. This is not founf in the "Gospel of Nicodemus". The English poet adds a freshness and wonder that is not found in the apocryphal scripture. He uses what he finds but is not afraid to change or add to the legendary material that are his sources.

    When Hell and Death saw Christ advancing into their realm, they cried out,

> 'Quat ert þu, þus es heder comen,
> Þu has vs in þi pouste nomen?
> Quat es þu þat es sua wight
> Vr schenschip forto scheu to dright? (44)   18172

Christ does not answer, but all the legions of devils, cringing like cowards as they are violently cast down, wail:

> 'QueÞen es þu sua seleuth a man,
> Sua mekil man, mighti and schene,
> And siÞin of all costes clene,
> For erdes werld þat has bene ay   18232
> vr vnderlute all to þis day,
> Þat agh vs rent of ȝong and ald,
> Bot neuer suilk als þis es ane
> Til vs ȝeit sent þai neuer nane.   18228
> Quat es þu þan þat es sua bald
> Comen þis wise intill be hald?
> Quatkin maistri mas þu on vs?
> Mai fall þu art þat ilk ihesus   18224
> Þat sathan vr prince vs of taldm
> And of þi dede on rode sua bald,
> Þat thoru þi dede apon þat tre,
> All þis werld suld bou to þe.' (45)   18220

The struggle between Christ and Satan is short. The "Gospel of Nicodemus" sums it up this way:

> Then did The King of Glory in his Majesty trample upon death, and laid hold on Satan the prince and delivered him into the power of Hell, and drew Adam to him unto his own brightness. (46)

The "Cursor" poet renders this passage thus:

> [w]id þis gan Iesus him to wreth
> Als þou he brath had bene in breth.
> Sathan, þat pinful prince, he light
> And vnder might of hell bitaght,
> Andadam tillward hedrogh, (47)

The poet does not develop ths combat between Christ and Satan as several writers do in the late Middle Ages. The conception of the Harrowing of Hell as a tournament in which Our Lord is man's "Champion" was particularily vital in England in the late fourteenth century, and it lies at the centre of some of the finest Medieveal poems about Redemption. (48) The "Cursor" poet's treatment of this episode is not so sophisticated as Langland's. (49)

The "Cursor" poet continues his narration with Hell mocking Satan for being conquered by Christ. All riches that Satan had won through Adam and his loss of Paradise, he had now lost through the Rood tree:

> All þat þu wan and mad þe rike
> Thoru adam and þe tre wid suike,   18268
> And thoru tining of paradise,
> Nu has þu tint on oþer-wise,
> Þu has tint thoru his rode tre,
> And gladschip all es gane fra þe. (50)   18264

Hell adds that Satan will feel many lasting pains while in his keeping.

Meanwhile, according to Carius and Lethius, eye-witness account of the events in the underworld when Christ decended into hell, Jesus inform Hell that Satan, instead of Adam and his brood, shall be under his power. He then turns to call on all the saints, damned through devil and a tree, to see a tree condemn the devil. These are Christ's words:

> 'Cum to me mj santes nu,

> All þat mi liknes has on ȝu,
> Cumes nu heder all to me,
> Þat thoru Þe warlou and a tre   18304
> All damoned war, nu sal ȝe se
> A tre did him to dampnes be,
> To dede ȝu deme he did sua dim
> Nu sal Þat dede be dampned on him.' (51)   18300

When all the saints were under the Lord's wing, Christ said to Adam, who was at his right hand:

> .,'adam i giue Þe Þes,
> To Þe and all childer Þine,
> And till all oÞer rightwis mine.' (52)

On hearing the joyful tidings, Adam and all the saints fall on their knees before Christ and sing songs of praise to Him. They refer to Our Lord as their "ransomer" who has set the mark of the cross on earth:

> '[N]u comen art Þu lauerd, vr dright,
> vr ransumer als Þu has hight,
> Þat Þu thoru prophete tald a[n]d tight
> Nu es fulfild bifor br sight,   18324
> Thoru Þi croice Þu has vs boght,
> And for vs has Þu hedir soght
> Fra dede of hell to lousen vs,
> All has Þi dede vs sauued Þus.'   18328
> 'Lauerd,' Þai said, all wid a steuen,
> 'Als Þu has sett Þi marke in heuen
> Of Þi blis lauerd god, sua gode,
> And has Þe taken of Þi rode   18332
> Raised in erd of ur ransun;
> Þu sett it lauerd in hell Þar dune,
> To knau Þi croice victori,
> Þat dede haue here na mare maistri.' (53)   18336

Thus the author clearly states that it was through Christ's victory on the Cross that death no longer had mastery over the souls of the just in hell.

Then Christ made the sign of the cross on Adam, blessed all of his saints, and taking Adam by the hand led him towards paradise. On the way, the blessed souls met with two old men who had never been in hell. They identify themselves as Enoch and Elijah, who never were dead, but are awaiting the coming of Antichrist, who is destined to slay them. Next, the joyful band of saints meet a miserable man carrying a cross. This is Dismas, the penitent theif. Christ grants him permission to go into paradise.

Carius and Lethius finish their strange and wonderful account of the Harrowing of Hell, saying that the archangel Michael commanded them to return to earth, where they were to be dumb. They end their narrative with a prayer.

> An dos ȝur penans quilis ȝe may:
> His pes be wid ȝu: a[n]d haues gode day." (54)

This version of the Kingdom of shadows is perfectly orthodox, despite its imaginary character. It is a popular presentation of the Christian faith in Christ's descent into hell. This faith is based on the fact that Christ died to redeem all men from their sin; owing to the fall of the first man their solidary in his sin had included all succeeding generations. If Christ came forth from the tomb victorious and overcame sin by his innocent death and freed mankind from the power of evil, then it was fitting that the first to benefit should be the souls of those just ones who had lived in hope of redemption. The liberation of the saints of the Old Testament is, then, only the natural consequence of the paschal mystery, of which St. Paul speaks, when in writing to the Ephesians, he tells them that Jesus, before ascending to heaven, "Had gone down, first to the lower regions of the earth." (55)

And what was the reason for Christ's visit to the underworld? "So that everything in heaven and on earth and under the earth must bend the knees before the name of Jesus, and every tongue must confree Jesus Christ the Lord, dwelling in the glory of God the Father." (56) When He proclaimed the Good News of Salvation to the Kingdom of the dead, Christ delivered the souls of the Devil and of death. He subjected all creation to His domination. St Paul alludes to Christ's descent into Hell in Romans 14.9: "That was why Christ's died and lived again; he would be Lord both of the dead and of the living."

The "Cursor Mundi" contains a vivid, dramatic description of Christ's Harrowing of Hell, of his binding of Satan, and of his deliverance of the Just from their long imprisonment there. The story of Christ's underworld mission is relyed by two men who are portrayed as having risen from the dead and who were in the realm of hell when Our Lord came. This results in a highly dramatic presentation that the poet skillfully links with early portions of his poem such as Seth's quest for the Oil of Mercy, and the history of the wood from which the true cross was made. William Henry Hulme s correct when he says:

> The literary account of Christ's descent into Hades was developed from a belief which doubtless prevailed in apostolical times that he descended into the underworld to preach, or to bring salvation, to the dead, just as he had brough salvation to the living by his mission on earth. (57)

The poet rounds out this episode with some details about Christ not found in his known sources. He informs us that Christ has thirty-two years, six months and two weeks old when He was put to death: that He lay two nights and one day in the grave. While Christ's body was in the tomb, His soul went to hell. His soul returned to His body after midnight on Easter morn. It is with these and similar details that the poet adds to the credibility of his account of the history of salvation,

Before he gives an account of Our Lord's life after He had risen, which is based mainly on the "Gospel of John" and "The

Acts of the Apostles", the "Cursor" poet gives a twenty-two line comparioson of Christ to a lion. This is based on an early Middle English Bestiary. It forms a fitting close for the secion of the "Cursor Mundi". In it, Christ is likened to a lion, who, when it is born lies dead three days, till his father roars at him and gives him life, so Jesus rose at his father's bidding. This is how the quaint conceit is developed:

> And alsua Þar es oÞer resun
> Qui he es takened to a leon, 18644
> Leon quelp quen it es born
> Liges dede to Þe thried morn,
> widvten lijf of anu lim,
> His [fadir] comis Þan to him; 18648
> And wid his cri Þat es sua greis,
> He giues his quelp lijf forto rijs.
> Sua did iesu, vr champioun,
> Þou he lai dede for vr ransoun, 18652
> Quen Þat his fader wald, he bad
> Þe sun vpras vs alle to glad. (58)

Chapter VII
The Finding of the Cross

The last section of the "Cursor Mundi" that centres around the Holy Rood legend that centres around the Holy Rood legend with the finding of the True Cross by Saint Helen in the fourth century of the Christian era. The "Cursor" poet further binds his long narrative by the inclusion of legendary material on the "invention", or discovery of the cross on which Jesus Christ was crucified. The story as it has Christ was crucified. The story as it has reached us has been admitted since the beginning of the fifth century by religious authors, with however, many more or less important variations. The tradition of the finding of the cross through the word of St. Helen, mother of Emperor Constantine, in the vicinity of Calvary was accepted as true by Cyril, Bishop of Jerusalem in 350, who was on the spot a very few years after the event took place. St. Ambrose bears witness to the fact of the finding.

Writers in the British Isles from the earliest times appear to have had a great interest in this legend. For example, Cynewulf, an eighth centry poet, wrote "Elene" – the story of the discovery of the true cross by the Empress Helena in old English. It was an accepted Medieval tradition that Saint Helen was the daughter of Coel of Caercolvin (Colchester). This would give an added interest in Britian to her life, the conversation of her son, and the finding of the cross. Alban Butler, (1711-73) the great hagiographer and the author of "The Lives of the Saints", states: "We are assured by the unanimous tradition of our English historians that this holy empress was a native of our island." (3) With regard to this legendary material, Haenich and other scholars have not succeeded in finding the sources have not succeeded in finding the sources that the "Cursor" poet might have used. The poet, as we have seen, prepares us for this in his narration of the events after Christ's death. After the crucifixion, Joseph of Arimathiae attempted to gain the possession of the cross on which Christ died. But the Jews refused buried it together with the crosses of the two robbers. This is how the author describes the hiding of the crosses:

> [I]oseph wald haue a-wai Þe rode,
> Þe iuus it him forbedd,
> Þat ilke night Þaim-self it did
> a-way for to be led;   16916
> wid Þe theifs croices tuin,
> quen all war gane to bedd,
> And groue Þaim thre for christen men,
> widin a preue stedd.   166920
> ForÞi Þai bar Þe maliscon
> of him Þat Þar-on bledd.

He concluded this passage with the significant remark, to which we will return in the next chapter, that when the cross was under earth and Christ was under stone, all the hope of the holy church hinged on the Blessed Virgin Mary;

> [N]u es Þe crois grauen vnder grete,
> and iesus vnder stane,   16924
> And hinges all hope of hali kire
> In mari mild allane. (5)

Some three thousand four hundred lines further on in the "Cursor Mundi", after the poet has described the important events of the apostolic times, he returns to the later history of the true cross:

> [O]F Þe rose nu for to rede
> Crist him-self vs do to spede! (6)   21348

Here he tells us that when Christ was taken off the cross the Jews hid it deep under the earth with those of the wo robbers, so that if found by chance men might not know which one of the three was the one on which Our Savior was crucified. The poet makes a point of the fact that the cross was found by means of a woman:

> A doghti wijf Þat hight eline,
> was moder of king Constantine. (7)

He also emphasizes the fact that he is beasing his account of the discovery on a well established source:

> Herkin, and i sal tell Þan you,
> [A]ls i in a stori it fand. (8)

This legend is similar in genre to many of the Medieval lives of the saints which contains many of the elements of the chivalric romance. (9) It balances the early history of the Holy Rood in the Old Testament times of King David and Solomon.

Here the "Cursor" poet fulfills the promise he made in his preface to deal with the finding of the cross:

> Of Þe hali crois hou it was kidd
> Lang efter Þat it was hidd; (10)   212

First we see the Roman emperor Constantine alone in his tent on the eve of a great battle. In a vision, the worried Constantine sees a marvelously fair man, who commands him to towards heaven and be comforted. The emperor does and sees:

> Sau he cristes crois ful bright;

> A titel sau he Þar-ley,
> "Herin," it said, "sal þu haue victori." (11) 21396

He caused a similar cross to be made and borne before him in the battle, and thus gained the day. Then he despatched two messengers, Benciras and Ansiers, (12) to Jerusalem to his mother Helen with instructions to try and find Christ's cross. She had, at that time, a Christian goldsmith with her who owed money to a Jew. According to the terms of the agreement, the goldsmith was either to repay the money or forfeit its weight of his own flesh. As he could not do the former, the Jew demanded the latter, and Constantines's messengers, who had now arrived in Jersalem, were called upon to give judgement. Their decision was that the Jew might take the money's weight of flesh, but must beware of spilling a single drop of blood.

The Jew, who has previously described which parts of the goldsmith's body he would take –

> His cien firist putt vte i sall,
> And his hend þat he wirkes wid-all, 21452
> Tung and nese, and siþen þe lau[e],
> Till þat i mi couenand haue." (13)

--with fiendish delight, is enraged at the adverse judgement and curses the emperor's messengers. This is a punishable offence. The Jew then offered to show Helen where Christ's cross was, if she would remit the penalty imposed on him. She grants his request.

This is a highly dramatic courtroom scene. By its inclusion, the poet has placed his narrative into the Medieval world. The question of usury and the Jew's position in society was a topical question at the time the "Cursor Mundi" was written. The Jewish community in York was massacred in 1290 and all Jews were expelled from England by the end of that century. The Medieval audience, who were familiar with tales of ritualistic murders of young Christians by Jews, would accept this Jew's inhuman cruelty in demanding his pound of flesh. In his handling of this section of the poem, the poet emphasizes the fact that he is not dealing with an event of ancient history. To Medieval man, the finding of the Cross was an event of ancient history. To Medieval man, the finding of the Cross was an event of recent history. It was commonly believed that Longius' spear that had lanced the side of Our Lord had been discovered at Antooch by the revelation of St. Andrew, in 1098, during the First Crusade. (14) The poet uses this episodes to show the importance of miracles in the post-apostolic age. It is also significant that this anglo-Jewish Medieval legend is combined with the legendary material dealing with the Holy Rood, which plays such an important part in strengthening the whole structure and framework of the "Cursor Mundi".

The poet now narrates the actual finding of the cross. Saint Helen, accompanies the Jew to the mount of Calvary on a certain day. The search is enlivened by a series of miraculous occurances. First when they had said their prayers, the earth quaked;

> Þan said Þe iuu, aad all it herd,
> "Crist Þu es sauueur of Þis erd !" (15)

Then the Jew, taking off all his clothes but 'sarke', took up a spade and began to dig. After going down more than twenty feet, he found three crosses. But they had no way of telling which of the three crosses was the one on which Christ died:

> He fand tua croices Þat ilke,
> Bot Þai wist noght quilk was quilke,
> Þe quilk might be Þe lauerd tre,
> And quilk it might Þe thefs be. (16)

The next miraculous event is when Helen orders that a dead man be brought and laid on each of the crosses. On touching the third cross, the corpse comes to life and worshipped the cross thus:

> "Godd Þe lock, crois, precius thing!

> In Þe hang alÞer heist king,
> Menskid wid his fless was Þu,
> Of alle tres most of vertu,   21556
> He was Þe halud Þat all can cene,
> And menskid wid all christen men;
> Thoru Þe has god sent nu me lijf,
> And thoru Þe worschip of Þis wijf." (17)   21560

The author remarks that many Jews witnessed this miracle, and as a result were baptized. The true Cross was then taken to the temple, where the remainder of the beam from which it had been made was discovered. A sweet odour from it filled the temple and a learned Jew informed the queen of the history of the royal tree. Helen then prayed to God to reveal to her what she should do with the cross, and an angel appeared and told her to cut it into four parts, of which one was to remain in the temple, the second to be brought to Rome, the third to be sent to Alexandria and the fourth to be taken to Constantinople. The queen did as she was directed and placed the fourth part personally in the Church of St. Sophia.

The miracles described in this episode balance the ones that appear in the early history of the wands and emphasize the fact that we are still living in an age in which God shows his supernatural powers to men. The "Cursor" poet summarizes the whole collection of myths and legends dealing with all aspects of the cross by a brief discussion of the mysteries that it represents. First the poet states that God gave us an example by the cross:

> [Þ]e grace of god es gret and gode,
> Þar gaue vs sampil bi ve rode,   21628

And then goes in to explain that many men will not believe the truth without signs:

> Bot mani of trouth es sua vnslie,
> Þei trou noght bot Þat pai se wid eie;   21632

> And Þat vnethes wil Þai trou,
> Widvten signe of gret vertu; (19)

Nevertheless, he maintain that the power and the influence of the cross has been apparent since the beginning of the world, and that if man were not blind he would see It in the old law as well as the new. He mentions Adam first:

> Had adam funden it at hand
> Þat wid Þe might had lijf lastand;
> Þat planted es in paradis,
> And dos Þe dede vp forto rise;   21652
> [A]nd adam wrought quen he had wogh,
> vnder Þis tre he him wid-drogh,
> Þar did him drightin for to reson
> And did him in hope of pardun. (20)   21656

Then Abel whose cry was in the cross:

> [Þ]e blod of abel it crid als
> Quen him had slan his broÞer a fals.
> wid Þat tre gret thing was hid,
> Þat in Þis ilk croice es hid,   21960
> And dede forsoth had bene noie
> If him ne sauued had Þe tre.

While Noah was saved by the cross and the ark had tokens of it:

> Of four querner Þe arche was made,
> Als had Þe crois on land and brad,   21664
> Þe dur of Þat arche apon Þe syide,
> And Þar was iesus wonde wide.
> Qua wil vmthinc him in his mode,
> Mai find fele takeins of Þe rode. (22)   21668

The significance of this symbol in the lives of Moses and David is explained. The rods of the twelve tribes were emblems of the cross.
 Turning to the Christian era, the poet remarks that the cross is the banner of Holy church:

> [C]roice es, qua-sum will or nai,
> Baner of hali kire to-day; 21720
> Men has noght herd Þat folk be lorn
> Þat hali croice has wid them born,
> Bot had bitid of mani quarem
> Þe less folk ouer-come Þe mare. 21724
> Þar croice was stad at ani fight,
> If Þat Þe dede be done wid right. (22)

It is also our medicine, sources of holy writ, foundation of the clergy and the command of the holy road:

> Þe croice of medicine beris bote,
> Bath in frut and alls in rote,
> In croice it was for vs Þe flour,
> Þat we haue thoru sua grett honur. 21736
> A riche licknes at beris itt,
> It es Þe heued of hali writ,
> Fundement f vr clergie,
> Reule es it als of hali vie. 21740

The symbol of the cross is vitally important in the history and redemption of man. The cross, according to the Catholic archaeologist P. Didron, is more than a figure of Christ; it is in iconography Christ Himself or His symbol. Didron states:

> Thus a legend had been created arounf it as if it were a living being; thus it has been made the hero of an epopee germinating in the Apocryphia; growing in the Golden Legend; unfolding and completeing itself in the works of

sculpture and painting from the 14th in the 16th centuries. (25)

In support of Didron's position, we have the Old English "Dream of the Rood", (26) which contains an address of the true cross to the poet, telling of the crucifixion and resurrection, and its reflection thereon. The poet may have worked from several sources simultanesously while writing this last section of the cross myth, which has almost become a protagonist during the long sections of the "Cursor Mundi". He invites anyone to improve on his narrative if they can. This is how he ends this important thread, which had run through close to twenty-two thousand lines of his monumental religious poem:

Of Þe croice es broght till ende,	
Þe vertu of Þe croice vs defend!	
Qua Þe tale can better attend	
For cristes luue he it amend.	21804
Þis, queÞer it be ill or gode,	
I fand it writen of Þe rode,	
Mani tellis diuersli,	
For Þai mai find diuers stori. (27)	21808

We must emphasize the fact that the "Cursor" poet did not merely graft the legendary of the cross onto the history of salvation. In his hands, the story is amplified and all the details are given a wonderful minuteness. IT is in his handling of this material we see his great skill as a story-teller. Also we must not lose sight of the fact that the chief object of the author of the "Cursor Mundi" as of many other medieval hagiologists was not to compose reliable histories or to write scientific treatises for the learned but to write works of devotion that were adapted to the simple manner of ordinary people. The work, we are certain, must have produced a deep impression on the Medieval audience for which it was intended. This can be seen in part as we have mentioned previously, by the unusually large number of manuscripts that have survived.

About the tenth century, the Fish disappeared as an important emblem used by Christians, and the Cross, an important symbol of our redemption from apostolic times, became the sole and universal sign of the Christian faith. St. Oaul in his epistle makes frequent allusios to the humiliation that Christ endured when he suffered death upon the cross. To the ancient Roman world it was a symbol of shame. Cicero says the very name of the Cross should be removed:

> not only from the body, but from the thoughts, the eyes, the ears, of Roman citizens, for all these things, not only the actual occurance and endurance, but the very contingeny and expectation, nay, the mention itself, are unworthy of a Roman citizen and a free man. (28)

It was precisely this idea that made the early Christians seize upon the cross as the emblem of their faith. That which has been the symbol of shame now became their glory. The instrument of Christ's passion, by His death upon it, became hallowed for all time. The Medieval Christians, desiring to see the cross identified still more closely with the fall of Adam and Eve inserted the legendary material concerning the Holy Rood to supplement the Old Testament.

The story, as the "Cursor poet remarks, has a large number of varying versions. All of the essential facts are included in this English version from the journey of Seth to the discovery of the true Cross by Saint Helen. Anna Jameson remarks:

> None of the old legends have been more universally diffused than the 'history of the True Cross': and I believe, that, till a darkness came over the minds of the people, it was, formerly as well understood in the allegorical sense as the "Pilgrim's Progress" is today. (29)

The most satisfactory and complete handling of the Holy Cross story in Middle English is found in the "Cursor Mundi". No essential part of the legend is omitted. Here the numerous threads of the various legends are knitted into a unified and pleasing whole.

The section of the Finding of the True Cross which we are examining in this chapter is often left out or treated separately. The "Cursor" poet's inclusion of it is a touch of genius. It helps to bring his account of divine history into the contemporary Medieval world. It would also please an English audience. For in cycle of our early Englis saints whenever they are to be found pictorially, either in old illuminated manscripts or in the decorations of old churches, Saint Helen, the mother of Constantine, and Saint Albin, our first martyr, take precedence over the rest. (30) A festival celebrated on May 3rd, (31) because on or about the day in 326 A.D. Helen is reputed to have discovered the true cross, was an important holy day in Medieval England. Pilgrims returning from Constantinople and Rome where there were important churches especially built to receive so precious a relic as part of Christ's cross, broght fragments of the sacred wood to England. It had been discovered that the wood exercised a power of miraculous self-multiplication, "ut detrimenta non sentiret, et quasi intacta permaneret" (Paulinus, Ep. XI ad Lev.) St. Cyril of Jerusalem, twenty-five years after the discovery, affirmed that pieces of the cross were spreading all over the earth, and compares this marvel to the miraculous feeding of five thousand men, as recorded in the Gospel.

Possibly the strangest innovation that the "Cursor" poet makes in his treatment of this material is his connection of the pound of flesh story, that anticipates the "Merchant of Venice" with his narrative of the finding of the Cross. He, however, integrates it well into his narrative. The "Cursor" poet does not express many anti-Semitic (32) views in this work. He includes the legend that the Jew who helped Helen find the Cross was converted to Christianity, and made bishop of Jerusalem. (33) The version of the Quiracus legend that the "Cursor" poet uses says that the devil threatened him with vengeance, but that

"crist, þat es lauerd mine,

> He deme Þe in to hell depe,
> Euer in welland wa to wepe." (34)   21836

Another possible reason for the "Cursor" poet's extensive treatment of this portion of the Cross legend may be due to Saint Helen's particular connection with the Benedictine Order, that had several important foundations in the South of Scotland in the thirteenth century. In the Middle Ages, it was belived that Saint Helen's remains had been carried off from Rose about the year 863, and were deposited in the Benedictine abbey of Hautvilliers in Champagne, France. Her beautiful but empty sepulchure can still be seen in Rome.

This episode of the Finding of the Cross fits in well into the general plan of the "Cursor Mundi". If we view this religious poem as an artistically composed work of devotion, we must admit that it is a complete success. It is admirably adapted to enhance our love and respect towards His blessed Mother, and, in the case of the episode examined in this chapter, to animate us with holy zeal to follow the example of the pious English St. Helen and have a firm faith in the power of the Holy Cross. The Medieval audience whould echo this prayer of the "Cursor" poet:

> [Þ]at hali croice i haue of red,
> Quar-apon iesu for vs was spredd,
> Be vr scheld and also vr spere
> Bituix vs and all helles here!   21840
> Stedfastli in hert to bere,
> For ilk day we wend in were,
> Ilk day in were we weind,
> Bot Þe, iesu! haue we na friend.   21844
> Thoru Þe croice make vs Þi friend.
> Thoru Þe croice make vs Þi friend
> To be vr succor at vr end. Amen. (35)

Chapter VIII

Recognition of our Lady's Role in the History of Salvation

In the preceding chapters of this work, we have examined the "Cursor" poet's careful use of legendary material dealing with the Oil of Mercy and the Holy Rood. In this chapter, we will briefly see the way in which he frames his poem in the Medieval devotion to Our Lady.

It is an accepted fact that Medieval poetry of the thirteenth and early fourteenth centuries was in a great meature orientated towards religion; it was the achievement of anonymous poets like the author of the "Cursor Mundi"

As indicated in Chapter II, the "Cursor Mundi" is framed in the devotion to the Blessed Virgin Mary, Mediatrux of Christ's redemption. The conclusion of the poem is merely a placing of the fruits and the reality of man's redemption within the contemporary Christian Church under the protection of Our Lady. This is dramatically indicated through the presentation of the wonderful and miraculous event surrounding the establishment of the feast of the conception of the Virgin Mary. (1) In the "Prologue", the poet announced that the last subject he intended to cover would be the conception of Our Lady:

The author, at the commencement of this monumental poem also stated that he was writing in honour of Mary:

[I]N hir worschip wald i biginne

>   A lastand werk apon to mine. 112
>   For to do men knaue hir kin
>   Þat us suilk worschip gan to win,
>   Sumkin ieste nu forto knau
>   Þat don was in Þe alde lau; 116
>   Bituix Þe ald lau and Þe new
>   Hu cristes bote bigan to brew,
>   I sal 3ou scheu wid min entent,
>   Sothli of hir testament 120

Though he indicated that before his work is finished, he will have dealt with some of the principle stories of salvation history—

>   All Þis werld, ar Þis boke bline,
>   Wid cristes help i sal our-rine,
>   And telle sum ieste principle, (4)

Let us now examine the position held by Christ's Mother during the late Middle Ages. The devotion to the Virgin Mary dates from the immediate post-apostolic times. It developed more rapidly in the East than in the West. Nevertheless, western Mariology during the early Medieval period rested largely on the achievements of the great Fathers, especially St. Ambrose and St. Augustine. The Greek influence becomes apparent in the works of St. Ambrose who died in 784. He was a Benedictine Abbot of a monastery near Benevento in Southern Italy, who strikes an entirely new note in Latin preaching on the Virgin Mary. He praises her because the world had been redeemed through her, the ladder by which God decended to earth; she is the door of heaven, the exaltation of apostles, the praise of martyrs, the jubilation of confessors. St. Ambrose asks Our Lasy to

> admit our prayers into the sanctuary of your hearing and bring us back the grace of reconciliation. Accept what we offer, obtain what we ask, protect us from what we fear:

because we find no one more powerful in merit to placate the wrath of the Judge than you, who have merited to be the mother of the Redeemer and Judge. (5)

The idea that the Virgin Mary appeases the wrath of God, the Judge, was to become one of the most important and popular themes of devotion to her during the Middle Ages. For as time passed, Christ was presented increasingly as the implicate Judge, and His Mother became the mediating power to whom Christians turned trustingly to save them from damnation, as she had been able to do in many medieval legends even in the case of those who had formally given their souls to the devil.

This emphasis on Our Lady's motherly mediation produced a change in her image in literature as well as in art. The Byzantine image of Mary was as the great "Theotokos", the Majestic, often even severe-looking Virgin who had given birth to God Himself.

In the West, the Virgin Mary was thought of as more "human. She was seen as above all a woman sharing the joys and the sufferings of women. If God, even the incarnate God, her Son, was still felt to be in some way remote from men, because He was a divine Person, Our Lady was wholly a mother, smiling at her Child, weeping at His sufferings and swonning at His death.

True, she was now enthroned in heaven;but she was in heaven also primarily as a mother, placed there to help her children struggling on earth. This is the image we get from reading many a Medieval sermon or peom. Here she is the gentle Mediatrix of all graces.

A proper understanding of Our Lady's position is vital for a deep comphrehension of the Medieval milieu. The "Cursor" poet shows us the central position she held in history of human salvation. The great men of the Renaissance of the twelfth and thirteenth centuries held the Mother of God in the highest esteem.

Henry Adams in his "Mon-Saint-Michel and Chartres",

brilllantly summarizes the result of the "cultus" of Mary:

> In the Western Church the Virgin had always been highly honoured. Her miracles became more frequent and her shrines more frewuented, so that Chartres, soon after 1100, was rich enough to build its western portal with Byzantine splendor. A proof of the new outburst can be read in the story of Citeaux. The Cistercian Order, which was founded in 1098, from the first put all its churches under the special protection of the Virgin, and Saint Bernard in his time was regarded as the apple of the Virgin's eye....

You can still read Bernard's hymns to the Virgin, and even his sermons, if you like. To him she was the great mediator. In the eyes of a culpable humanity, Christ was too subime, too terrible, too just, but not even the weakest human frailty could fear to approach his Mother. Her attribute was humility; her love and pity were infinite. "Let him deny your Mercy who can say that he has ever asked in vain." (6)

The permanence of Medieval man's devotion to Our Lady can be seen today in such works as the "Cursor Mundi" or the sculpture, mosaic, painting of great churches of the thirteenth and fourteenth centuries. The importance of the Virgin Mary cannot be emphasized too strongly in the period between the first Crusade (1096) and the Black Death (1349). But we will content ourselves with one more quotation from Henry Adams before investigating how the "Cursor" poet used Our Lady to frame his religious epic:

> According to statistics, in the single century between 1170 and 1270, the French built eighty cathedrals and nearly five hundred churches of the Cathedral class, which would have cost, according to an estimate made in 1840, more than five thousand million to replace. Five thousand mil-

lion franc is a thousand million dollars, and this covered only the great churches of a single century.... The share of this capital which was – if only may use a commercial figure – invested in the Virgin cannot be fixed, any more than the toal sum given to religu=ious objects between 1000 and 1300; but in a spiritual and artistic sense, it was almost the whole, and expressed an intensity of conviction never again reached by any passion, whether of religion, of loyalty, of patriotism, or of wealth, perhaps never paralleled by any single economic effort except in war. Nearly every great church of the twelfth and thirteenth centuries belonged to Mary.... But, not satisfied with this, she contracted the habit of requiring in all churches a chapel of her own, called in English the "Lady Chapel", which was apt to be as large as the church but was always meant to be handsomer. (7)

This was the religious climate the Medieval man knew.

In dealin with the Old Testament, the poet points out that he is showing who the Virgin Mary's forebearers were. In this section of the work he makes a conscious effort to tie happenings in other parts of the world to his narrative. He thus shows the all-embracing importance of events of Jewish history in mankind's existence on earth. He tells us Troy was built, (8) and that Helen was alive at this time. (9) He mentions that Troy was destroyed by the Greeks after ten years of siege. (10) He remarks that in King David's time, Homer flourished, and Carthage was founded by that strong baronage of Africa that was ever hostile to Rome. (11) The poet notes other important dates such as these. Some are found in his sources such as Peter Comestor's "Historia Scholastica", but often he expounds them to make them more significant.

We are never allowed to forget the total world picture in any portion of the poem. The poet, by these references to events in other parts of the world, gives his work a genuine flavor of the world, gives his work a genuine flavour of a worldy history or chronicle. He joins these events in other parts of the world, gives his work a genuine flavor of a worldly history or chronicle. He joins these events of secular history to his account of the supernatural intervention of the Creator in the lives of men. The Blessed Vurgin, who is wholly human, is a strong link between the narrative of human redemption and the facts of secular history. The poet devotes a long section to telling of her parents, conception and childhood. This section of the "Cursor Mundi" is balanced by the equally long account of the wonderful Childhood of Christ. The first section emphasizes the fact that Our Lady was just an ordinary Jewish maiden whom God had selected to be the vessel to bear His Son. The latter section highlights the divine nature of Christ. The role of the Virgin Mary during the life-time of her Son was that of a gentle, loving mother. The poet in his harmony of the Gospel does not draw our attention to her. She only takes the centre of the stage, so to speak, at the crucifixion. The dying Christ speaks to Mary:

> Iesus Þan sau his modir wepe,
> Of hir he had gret pete,   16756
> "Modir, iohn sal be Þi sun
> fra nu, instead of me.
> And Þi modir, mi dere cosin,
> Þu loke hir hir," said he,   16760
> Fra Þan he his leuedi lagh[t]
> in his ward for to be. (12)

She was among the few who remained steadfast to Christ. The poet says he does not possess the power to describe Mary's sorrow when she received the mangled and bloody corpse from Joseph of Arimathiae and Nicodemus, who took it from the cross:

> [Þ]e murning Þat his moÞer made
> main a man rede in rune. (13)   16880

All during the Middle Ages thre was popular veneration of the Virgin Mary on Saturdays. This practice, which was widespread in the west in the ninth century, appears to have grown out of the ancient weekly memorial of Christ's Passion. With regard to this custom, Father Francis X. Weiser, S.J., states:

> The books of that time motivate it by te thought that while the Lord's body rested in death, Mary alone did not doubt or despair, but firly adhered to the faith in her Divine Son. (14)

The "Cursor" poet makes reference to this Medievel belief:

> [N]u es Þe crois grauen vnder grete,
> and iesus vnder stane,   16924
> And hinges all hope of hali kire
> in mari mild allane. (15)

And the poet returns to this belief later on:

> [I]n Þe Þan, leuedi, hang all
> vr trouth and fai,   17068
> All men was in dute and were
> bot Þu, leue hali mai!
> Til Þi suete sun vp-ras
> Þi trouth was stabil ai,   17072
> Hu men agh vr lauerd leue,
> Þu lered vs Þar Þe wai.
> [M]ari meke, Þu mode res,
> ful of reuth and pete.   17076
> Mirthful maiden, mild of all!
> fulfild of all bunte. (16)

Our Lady was thus believed to deserve more devotion and honour on Saturdays than on other days of the week. The authorities of the Church not only provided a votive mass, but also a special Officed in honour of Mary, to be recuted on "free" Saturdays.

At the beginning of his account of the Assumption of Our Lady, the poet indefatigably says that he is Mary's slave:

> Þou nan als i be sua vnworthi man,
> Hi????am wid all Þat i can,   20016
> wid fell and fless and saule wid-all,
> I am and euer sal be hir thrall;
> For i am neuer mare sua fre
> Als till Þat leuedi thralled be. (17)   20020

She appears to be the inspiration for the whole of the "Cursor Mundi". Here the poet also states that any person who devoutly hears or reads this book will receive Our Lady's blessing and the remission of his sins. He has an abiding faith in Our Lady's power and Mercy:

> I witt ȝu to say widvten were,
> Þat all Þat hertli wil it here,   20044
> Hertli heris it or redis,
> Þai sal haue hir blissing to medis,
> Bath cristes aun benison
> And of Þair sines remissium;   20048
> Womman sal noght peris of barn,
> Ne nane wid mistime be forfarn
> Ne fall in-to na dedeli plight,
> Quen Þai it here, dai or night,   20052
> And mar Þar-of i sal ȝu ȝeit,
> Qua hertli redis or heris it,
> Of vr leuedi and saint iohn,
> Þair beniscon Þaim bes boght won. (18)   20056

The poet then mentions that Saint Edmund of Pontenay (19) has granted forty days' pardon for reading and hearing the history of salvation. Here again the "Cursor" poet re-affirmed the remark he made in his "Prologue" that his poem is intended for the ordinary people who understand English.

Concerning the story of Our Lady's death, he says that it was writeen in southern English, which he has turned into the northern dialect:

> In suthrin englijs was it draun,
> And i haue turned it till vr sun
> Langage of Þe norÞren lede,
> Þat cana nan oÞer englis rede. (20)   20064

This section is transcribed from the "South English Legendary", (21) written by an unknown English poet a few years before the "Cursor Mundi". The date of composition for the lengthy collection of lives of saints is usually give as about 1285.

Just as in the account of Our Lady's Childhood, the "Cursor" poet does not hurry over her last days on earth and burial. He tells again how Christ put the Virgin Mary under the protection of Saint John before he died, and how John faithfully served her. He goes on to tell how Our Lady became a nun in the temple, doing such works of charity that all loved her. After she had been there for a long time, her Son sent an angel to her to inform her that she would join Him in Heaven in three days. The angel greeted her as "Flour of erd, of hevn quene, Blissed mote Þou ever bene!" (22) while giving her a palm as a token from Christ. The angel then visits the apostles scattered across the world to inform them of Our Lady's imminent death. The poet adds a homely feminine touch when he has Mary put on new clothes:

> And quen Þat leuedi sua had done,
> A neu smoke scho did hir on. (23)

Our Lady then prays that Christ will keep her from Pain, shame and the devil; and to give men whom He had bought, amendment, so as not to fear the devil. The apostles are miraculously all brought to Jerusalem, and salute Mary as the "Queen of Heaven". Our Lady's last request is that the apostles watch over her body, not letting those who slew her sone get hold of it when her soiul has departed for heaven.

The earth quakes as Chris and His singing angels come to Mary's bower. Out Lady knew her Son and blessed Him. Christ replies:

> "Suete moÞer, Þu cum to me,
> Of all wimmen best ȝe be,
> Þar i am king Þu sal be quene,
> Ful blith Þan mai Þi her tai bene." (24)   29604

The poet continues his narration of Our Lady's passing and the miracles that attended her funeral in a leisurely fashion. This whole section of the work covers a total of eight hundred lines. He concludes by quoting St. Jerome, who questioned the bodily assumption of the Blessed Virgin Mary. But the poet adds that this is not so important as is the fact that Mary, empress of heaven and earth, and never stops praying for sinful man:

> Bot wele wa wate, widuten wene,
> Of heuen and erd Þat scho es quene,   20800
> Bath emperice of heuene, leuedi
> Sett in throne hir dere sun bi. (25)

According to the poet's reckoning, Our Lady was sixty-three years of age at the time of her death.

The "Cursor" poet freely manipulates his sources, now to stir his audience by violence, now to move them to piyu, and now to charm them with lyric beauty. The narrative pace of this enormous work with epic proportions rarelty flags. The "Cursor Mundi" is sometimes prolix, but only when it suits the poet's purpose to be so. He is seldom long-winded. The very matter that he had chosen to write about – the story of man's redemption – demands a solemn movement from one vital incident to the next. The poet moves majestically down through the ages, using legends such as the Oil of Mercy and the history of the Holy Rood to hold the interest of his audience. There is a steady and relentless unfolding of divine history. The poem is rarely vague, and there are many homely references and little touches of humour. Dramatic dialogue is rarely used; the poet saves it for the climaxes of his work. The short rhyming couplets (26) are well suited to this long religious poem, which in many places is as exciting as any Medieval romance.

    The author of the "Cursor Mundi" makes only one personal reference in the twenty-five thousand lines. After giving a lengthy description of what will happen at the end of the world, "the Day of Doom", the poet returns to the present with a prayer to the Virgin Mary that begins thus:

> [L]Euedi! loke to Þis caitiue clerk,
> For-sake Þu noght Þis roide werk,
> For Þou it roid and stubil be,
> It es in worschip wrought of Þe. (27)   23912

This would indicate that the poet was some "wretched clerk" in a large monastic institution. The language of his appeal to the "Englis lede of mer ingeland" and the way in which he presents his matter echo the tone and level of such contemporary works as the "South English Legendary". The "Cursor" poet seems to have been someone regularly employed in the instruction of the faithful. We feel, however, that Laurel Braswell is wrong when she insists that the poet must have been a parish priest. (28)

    The above prayer is the opening of the last large division of the "Cursor Mundi". The poet, whose interest in his work never appears to have slackened, uses a change in pace as he describes the Sorrows of Mary. (29) Here, for the second time only he changes his verse from rhyming couplets to stanzas of six lines. (30)

This section is writte in the form of a dialogue between the poet and the Blessed Virgin. This seven hundred-line poem restates the suffering and death of Christ as it would have been seen through the eyes of His mother. This is most moving part of the poem. For example when Our Lady compares Christ of former days with Christ hanging on the Cross:

> Fair he wes and fre, mi child,
> Softe in speche, in maner mild,
> Quil he stod in his state;
> His face þat fo[r]wit was sa schen,   24080
> It es nou grisly on to sen,
> His bodu al blodi wate. (31)

The "Cursor" poet also has Our Lady say that she was so sick she could not get out of bed to see her Son after He rose from the dead:

> [S]ua seke i was and sar for soruu,
> Quen mi sun ras þe third moru,   24636
> All till his graue þai thrang,
> Might i noght diderward a fote,
> Ne forto bid me was na bote,
> Þat let thoght me ful lang."   24640

He goes on to say that now Our Lady's sorrow is lightened because she is with Christ in eternal bliss, and asks her to help us.

After a brief apostrophe to Saint John, the poet commences the final section of the "Cursor Mundi", which deals with the establishement of the Festival of Mary's conception. He thus takes a contemporary miracle to end his monumental religious epic to show us that Our Lady still watches over and protects her own. He appears to be conscious that he has talked too much, but defends it by saying that nothing can be too that honours the Virgin Mary:

> [L]istes gode men, wid ȝur leue
> Ful lath me war ȝu forto greue,
> Þat ȝu thoght nu talking togh,
> For me thinc neuer mar enogh,   24736
> Þat i mai of hir louing rede,
> Þat bett vs all vte for vr need. (33)

 This charming legend with which the "Cursor" poet ends his poem had wide currency in the Middle Ages. It was one of the few strictly English legends that appeared in the "Legenda aurea". The poet's immediate source appears to be Wace's "The Establishment of the Feast of the Conception". One unique feature of the "Cursor" poet's handling of the story in his reference to William the Conquerer as "William Bastard". (34)

 The legend deals with a vision seen by Helsin, the abbot of the Benedictine abbey at Ramsey in 1070, while he was in a storm at sea. There was a historical person called Helsin, who was one of the councilors to William I, and who was sent by him to the King of Denmark with gifts when that foreign monarch threatened to invade England to revenge the death of his cousin, Harold, at the battle of Hastings.

 The "Cursor" poet takes delight in describing how William conquered the English:

> [A] king þat hight wihiam bastard,
> Þat werraid ingland ful hard,
> Su???? Stalworth man he was of hand,
> Þat wid his fors he wan þe land.
> Ful seleuth keneli cuth he fight,
> He slogh þe king þat herald hight,
> Þat born was of þe dancs blod,
> For-qui þe land he him wid-stode.   24772

> Þan bar wiliam Þe seyhnuri
> Of ingland and of normundi. (35)

He dwells longer on the earlier part of the story and his version contains many details not found in other treatment of this legend. For example, he explains the reasons why the Danish King threatened to invade England:

> ye king of danmark on-ane
> Herd Þat king herald was slane,   24776
> Of witt al-mast wald he weind,
> For luue of harald his friend.
> Schippis did he dight him ȝare
> In-till ingland Þan for to fare,   24780
> Apon Þe normandes forto fight,
> Þat wan Þe land widuten right;
> For he suar bi Þe king of heuen,
> Þat herald slaghter suld he heuen. (36)   24784

He also describes Willliam's consternation at hearing this news and the steps he took to combat the threatened invasion of England:

> To king willam bodword was broght
> Of Þis tiÞand Þat him forthoght,
> He dred him sare Þat were suld rise,
> And warnist him on mani wise;   24788
> He gedrid souders here and Þare,
> To strenth his castelis eueray quar,
> Als he Þat conqueror was gode,
> And for to werrai vnderstode.   24792
> His consail bad him for to fand,
> Þe king of danemark widstand,
> For to speke of sumkon pais,
> Bituix him and Þaa da[na]is. (37)   24796

William is guided by the advice of his councilors, and sends the Abbot of Ramsay on a peace mission. Helson, whose name would indicate that he was of Norse descent, was one of the few Englishmen to hold a high position in the court of the Conqueror. The mitred abbot is described by the "Cursor" poet as:

> A heind man and a wis; 24800
> A grete resun wele schau he cuth,
> Widvten ani maring in muth.
> Þis abbot of Þis erand bere,
> was chosin to be messa[g]ere. 24804
> vnto dane-mark to fare,
> Als man was lerid of mekil lare.

Thus skillfully the poet brings his work into his own day. The character of Helsin, well-known historical figure, is given concreteness. He bears "gold" and "silver" gifts to placate the Danish Monarch, and being a clever politician he does not forget to give presents to important people at the Danish court:

> Till erlis and baruns of Þat rike,
> Þan gaue he sere giftes eke;
> Þaa Þat he had na giftes till,
> wid hightes faure he went Þair will. 24824
> Sua wele in speche cuth he spell,
> Þat all Þat ost he did to duell. (39)

The peace mission was a complete success, and after in turn receiving gifts from the Danish King, the Abbot of Ramsey set sail once more for England. (40) But no sooner had the ship put out to sea than a violent storm arose:

> Þe wedir als in somer smeth
> Sone bigan it ruth and reth,

> Þat ilk wau til oÞer weft,
> And bremli to Þat barge beft.   24840
> Þe lift it blakind al to night,
> On illke side Þaim slaked sight
> Þe see for rethnes wex al rede,
> To dole was turned al Þair nede. (41)   24844

There then follows a graphic description of the storm, which is written in the best tradition of Middle English verse:

> Þe wind ras gain Þaim ful vnride,
> Þe Þaim sailed on ilk side.
> Þaim bleu mani vnrekind brast,   24848
> Strangli straite Þan war Þai stadd,
> Þe marinelis war selcuth radd,
> Sua rad ne war Þai neuer are,
> For Þai war neuer in perel mare. (42)   24852

All fear that they will drown. They pray to the Virgin Mary to come to their aid. Our Lady cannot refuse them and sends an angel, who tells Helsin that if he promises to establish a feast in honour of Mary's conception, all will be saved:

> Nou sal Þu hight and vou me here,   24890
> Þat Þu sal do als i Þe say
> Till all Þe kirkes Þat Þu may.
> Quen Þu come into ingland
> Forto do Þaim at vnderstand,   24894
> Forto halu Þis ilke dai
> wid all Þe worschip Þat Þai may;
> In hali kirke rinand bi ȝere,
> Als getin was vr leuedi dere   24898
> Geten was scho all to be born,
> Forto sauue all Þat war lorn.
> Þis es Þe day als scho was getin,

Loke it neuer mar be forgetin; (43) 24902

The abbot is only too pleased to promise. He then asks the angel what service should be used, and is told to use the same one as is used on the eight of September, the Nativity of Our Lady. The poet here remarks that:

>   Bot nu it es on oþer wise
>   Þar es made of prope seruise, 24932
>   Þat qua sua will nu may say,
>   Proper of þat concepcion day. (44)

As soon as Helsin makes his vow, the angel disappears and the storm abates and the vessel makes a safe passage to England. The abbot keeps his word, and the feast soon became one of the most popular in the calendar. The account of the Abbot of Ramsey's vision found its way into the Roman Breviary by 1473.

The "Cursor" poet, after finishing this delightful legend, which strengthens his theme concerning Our Lady, ends his poem quickly. He concludes with a prayer:

>   Þe stori þar-wid forto say,
>   Euern quan we will hald þis day, 24964
>   Mai na man serue hire in lede,
>   Þat scho ne ʒeildes þaim þar mede.
>   Scho do vs here at serue hir sua,
>   Þat we be wid hir euer and a. Amen. (45) 24968

This tale telling of the institution of the festival of Mary's conception balences the "Prologue" and tightens the whole of this long religious epic by giving it a narrow border. The poet indicates that we are still living in the age of miracles, in the time of Grace before the Second Coming of Christ. The Blessed Virgin Mary, the Mother of Our Saviour, in whose honour the poet has written this poem, is the only sure advocate that we poor sinners have.

Chapter IX
Conclusion

The problem we have set ourselves in this work is the examination of the narrative unity of the "Cursor Mundi". This twenty-five thousand line poem, written in the northern dialect of Middle English, is thought to have been composed in the Lowlands of Scotland in about year 1300. This poem has often because of its title been incorrectly regarded by critics as a rambling accumulation of Bible stories and legends. This is not so: a careful examination of the text as found in the fourteenth century Göttingen manuscript clearly revealed that the "Cursor" poet skillfully selected and combined various elements to fashion a narrative of man's salvation. The "Cursor" poet skillfully combines straightforward Bible accounts with apocryphal myths and legends – some of which are here for the first time found in English. He also gives unity to his work by framing the "Cursor Mundi" in tender devotion to Our Lady.

The "Cursor Mundi" is one of the most ambitious religious poems undertaken in the British Isles in the Middle Ages, and is also one of the most successful in execution. It is one of the many works that resulted from the decrees of the Fourth Lateran Council and the consequent didactic revival. It appears to have been written for both the clergy and laity who were not fluent in French. The "Cursor" poet clearly states his aims in his short "Prologue": to make the account of man's fall and redemption as interesting and as readable as possible; and to increase devotion to

Our Lady in whose honour the work has been written.

In our examination of the structure of the poem, most attention has been given to the use of the apocryphal stories of the oil of mercy and the myths of the wands that became the tree of the cross.

We have discovered the tight dramatic merging of myth and prophecy in the central great episodes of the salvation epic: the crucifixtion and the harrowing of hell.

The poem touches Medieval man closely as it continues into the later history of the cross as it continues into the later history of the cross and ends with a courteous establishment of the feast of her conception.

Notes

Introduction

1. "Cursor Mundi". G. 11. 20062-64. These lines do not appear in the Midland manuscripts, Trinity and Laud, but do appear in Cotton, Edinburgh, Göttingen and Fairfax. The latter is from Lancashire and is considered "nothrin" in contrast to the "sotherin" (Midland) of the Assumption Fragment, 11. 20065-848. In this work we will quote as far as possible from the Göttingen manuscript as it is the oldest, being 14th century. The Cotton manuscript is end of 14th century and beginning of 15th century. See. J.E. Wells, "A Manual of the Writing in Middle English 1050-1400" (London, 1916), pp. 399-40.
2. James A. H. Murray, "The Dialect of the Southern Counties of Scotland" (London, 1873), p. 30. (Durham).
   Max Kaluza, "Zu den Quellen und dem Hss-Verhaltnis des 'Cursor Mundi'", "Englische Studien", XII (1888), p. 453. (Nordlich vom Tweed).
   Heinrich Hupe, "Cursor Studies and Criticism on the Dialects of MSS" (1888) p. 186. (Lincolnshire).
   Otto Strandburg, "The Rime-Vowels of Cursor Mundi", Uppsala Diss., (1919), p. XV. (Northumberland).
   Rolf Kaiser, "Zur Geographie des mittelenglischen Wortschatzes". Palaestra 205 (Leipzig, 1937), p. 8. (Scotland).

Jacob J. Lamberts, "The Dialect of Cursor Mundi" (Cotton MS Vespasian A III), Michigan Dissertation, (1954), p. 2. (Scotland).

J.A.W. Bennett, "Early Middle English Verse and Prose", (London, 1966), p. 365. (Scotland).
3. With regard to this city, it is worth mentioning that chronicle writing was particularly that chronicle writing was particularly associated with the Benedictine Order. The cathedral of St. Cuthbert, Durham, was associated with his religious order. In the 14th century Durham boasted the largest library in the British Isles, and was famous for the copying of manuscripts. (See J. Stranks, "Durham Cathedral" (London, 1960), p. 23.)
4. "Cursor Mundi", G. 11. 231-250
5. Strandberg, op. cit., p. XIV.
6. O.F. Emerson, "The History of the English Language" (New York, 1897), p. 100. The same argument is used by Rolf Kaiser, op. cit., p. 8. Also Murray, op. cit., pp. 41-42: "Down to the end of the 15th century, there was no idea of calling the tongue of the Lowlands 'Scotch'; whenever the 'Scottish language' was spoken of, what was meant was Gaelic or Erse, the tongue of the original Scots, who gave their name to the country. The tongue of the Lowlanders was 'Inglis', not only as having been the tongue of the Angles of Lothian and Tweeddale, and as having been introduced beyond the Forth by Anglo-Saxon settlers, but English as being the spoken tongue of the northern subjects of the King of England, those with whom the subjects of the King of Scotland came most immediately in contact."
7. For example, in the "Legenda aurea"'s version of this story William is referred to as 'the glorious Duc of Normandy'. See: William Caxton, "The Golden Legend" (Kelmscott Press, 1892), pp. 236-37, and also "Mirk's Festial", ed. Theodore Erbe, EETS. os 96 (London,

1905) p. 17.
8. Murray, op. cit., p. 30.
9. Lamberts believes this Manuscript to have been written ca. 1400 in or near Durham, which must be distinguished from the original poem, composed ca. 1300 in Southern Scotland. See his unpublished dissertation for his argument. (Michigan, 1954).
10. Hupé, op cit., pp. 186-89. Hupé *settles on Lincolnshire because it enables him to explain the name of John of Lindberg which occurs in the* Göttingen manuscript line 17100: "John of Lindberghe, i zu sai Þat es mi name ful right". He then identifies this name with a Lincolnshire man, having made up his mind regarding the date before he begins examining the evidence.
11. *Robert Grosseteste, bishop of Lincoln and one of the most learned men of his age, died on 9 October, 1253. There were several attempts to procure his canonization (see the letter of Archbishop Romanus to Pope Honorius IV in 1287, and of Archbishop Greenfield to Pope Clement V in 1307, Raine, "Letters from Nothern Registers", pp. 87, 182, and that of the dean and chapter of St. Paul's to Pope Clement V in 1307, Warton, "Anglia Sacra", ii, 343)*
12. Strandbert, op. cit., p. XIV.
13. "Altenglische Metrik I" (Bonn, 1881), p. 265.
14. See: Haenisch, "Inquiry into the Sources of the Cursor Mundi", EETS, os. 99 (London, 1892), pp. 1-56.
    L. Borland, "Herman's Bible and the 'Cursor Mundi'", "Stud. Phil." XXX (1933), 427.
    L. D'Evelyn, "Methodius as Source", PMLA XXXIII (1918), 147.
    P. Beichner, "The 'Cursor Mundi' and Petrus Riga". "Speculum," XXIV (1949), 239.
15. Haenish does not suggest any source for lines 24970-29555, evidently not considering it proper to the "Cursor Mundi". Richard Morris points out (Pref. p. IX) that

this material appears only in the northern copies. The poet himself remarks lines 219-220: "Þe last resun of alle Þis run/sal be of her concepcion", suggesting that the additions may be merely other poems by the same author or a contribution by a later writer. Strandberg accordingly concludes his investigations at line 24970.
16. See: Cursor Mundi", G. 11. 23879-84, in which the poet says he is one of the unworthy shepherds whom Christ has set to feed his sheep; and line 23909: "Leudi! loke to Þis caitive clerk", (Lady, look at this wretched clerk).
17. The surviving manuscripts are:
Cambridge, University Library, MS. G8. 4, 27, 2.
Edinburgh, Royal College of Physicians.
London, British Museum, Cotton MS
Vespasian A. III.
London, British Museum, MS. Additional 10, 036.
Gottengen, University Library, MS. Theol. 107.
Oxford, Bodleian Library, Fairfax MS. 14.
Cambridge, Trinity College, MS. R. 3. 8.
London, British Museum, Herald's College MS., Arundel Press, 57.
London, British Musuem, Bedford MS. 9
(Now MS. Additional 36, 983.)
18. "Cursor Mundi, a Northumberkand Poem of the XIVth Century", 4 versions, ed. Richard Morris EETS os. 57, 59, 62, 66, 99, 101 (London, 1874-93). The Manuscripts used by Morris are Cotton MS.; Vespasian A III; Fairfax MS. 14; Göttingen MS. Theol. 107; and Trinity College MS. R. 3. 8.
19. Barth, op, cit., pp. 10-13.
20. Kaiser, op. cit., p. 7, raises a question about this and suggests line 11000 as perhaps more exact.
21. See the illustrations in the "Eadwin Psalter". Also C.R. Dodwell, "The Canterbury School of Illuminations 1066-1200" (Cambridge, 1954).

Chapter I: The Contemporary Milieu of the Cursor Mundi

1. See R. G. Collingwood, "The Idea of History" (London, 1946), pp. 46-56.
2. See Jean Danielou, "The Lord of History" (London, 1958), pp. 1-3.
3. St. Augustine, "The City of God", XXII, 30 (New York, 1950), p. 492.
4. See Genesis 5:1, and Matthew 1:1-17.
5. See "Cursor Mundi", G. 11. 9197-9.
6. Ranulf Higden, "Polycronicon", Trans. Trevisa, I. 31.
7. V.A. Kolve, "The Play Called Corpus Christi" (Stanford, 1966), pp. 118-19.
8. Erich Auerbach, "Figura", trans. Ralph Manheim, in "Scene from the Drama of European Literature (New York, 1959), p. 72.
9. For a discussion of time with regard to the Mystery Cycles see:
   H. Craig, "English Religious Drama", p. 16;
   Klive, "The Play Called Corpus Christi". pp. 101-123.
10. "Middle English Sermons", ed. Woodburn O. Ross, EETS os. 209 (London, 1940), pp. 112-13.
11. See Jacopo de Voragine, "Legenda aurea", I, 13.
12. See C.R. Cheney, "English Synodalia of the Thirteenth Century", (Oxford, 1941), p. 121.
13. See Laural Braswell, "The South English Legendary Collection", Unpublished Dissertation (Toronto, 1964), p. 20.
14. The only manuscript that has been printed in full is Laud 108, dating 1275-90. It is edited by C. Hortsmann EETS. 87 (London, 1887). For a discussion of the possible influence of the "Legenda aurea" on the English collection see Minnie E. Wells, "The South English Lengedary" in its relation to the 'Legenda aurea'" PMLA, LI (1936), 337-360.

15. See Braswell, op. cit., pp. 5-8.
16. See "Cambridge Medieval History", Vol. VI, 744.
17. See L. Stevenson, "Robert Grossesteté, Bishop of Lincoln", (Londom, 1899), p. 101.
18. Just who did the adapting is still in question. M.D. Legge, "Anglo-Norman in the Cloisters" (Edinburgh, 1950), p. 108, suggests that Robert Grossesteté originated the work.
19. Robert of Brunne's "Handlying Synne", ed. Frederick J. Furnivall, EETS 172, 123, (London, 1901-03), vv. 37-52, 7, 408-13 and 10804-7.
20. "Cursor Mundi", G. II. 237-40.
21. See "Early English Homilies", ed. R.D.N. Walker, EETS os. 152 (London, 1917) and "The Blicking Homilies" ed. Richard Morris, EETS os. 73 (London, 1880)
22. See R.W. Chambers, "Continuity of English Prose from Alfred to More and his School". Introduction to Nicholas Harpsfield, "Life of Sir Thomas More", EETS os. 186, (London, 1932).
23. Jocelyn of Brakelond, "Chronica" in "Memorials od Saint Edmund's Abbey". Rolls Series 16 (London, 1890). pp. 244-5. Rolls Series 16 (London, 1890). pp. 244-5.
24. Edited by Robert Holt, 2 Vols. (Oxford, 1878).
25. The "Ormulum" is the greatest value to the Middle English philologist in indicating for us the quality of the vowels in the many words which it contains.
26. See Marion T.H. Aitken, "Etude sur 'le Miroir de Robert Gretham'" (Paris, 1922)
27. See Margaret Deansly, "The Lollard Bible" (Cambridge, 1920). p. 150.
28. The lives of saints are liturgical because they developed from notes in church calendars that were used for homilies as part of the religious services.
29. See Braswell, p. 18
30. "Cursor Mundi", G. I. 21830 ff.

31. See Braswell, p. 22
32. "The South English Legendary" is exstant in 51 manuscripts. Parts of it have been edited in "The Early South English Legendary", ed. Carl Hortsmann. EETS os. 169 (London, 1927); and "The South English Legendary", ed. Charlotte d'Evelyn and Anna Jean Mill. EETS os. 236 (London, 1956 for 1951-2).
(This is a combination of Latin, Old English, and Anglo-Norman saints' legends, arranged chronologically according to the liturgical year. It is the first cycle of saints' lives to appear in Middle English.)
33. The "North English Homily Collection" has been only edited in fragment. See J.E. Wells, "Manual", pp. 287-92.
34. See Kolve, pp. 57-100. His remarks concerning the Mystery Cycles are also applicable to the "Cursor Mundi".
35. See Kolve, pp. 57-100. His remarks concerning the Mystery Cycles are also applicable to the "Cursor Mundi".
36. Parts II-V, edited, respectively, by Otto Moldenhauer, Hans Burkowitz, Eugen Kremers, and Ernst Martin, Series of University of Greifswald dissertations, appeared in 1914. Other titles for this twelfth century poem in the dialect of Piccardy, are: "Li Livres de la Bible", "Bible de sapience", "historie de la Bible", and "Roman de sapience".
37. Ed. par Mancel et Trebutien (Caen, 1842).
38. The French original was printed and published by the Caston Society, ed. by M. Cooke (London, 1852).
(It is some 1750 lines in length.)
39. "The Apocryphal New Testament", Trans. by M.R. James, (Oxford, 1924). pp. 70-79.
40. "The Apocryphal New Testament", Trans. by. M.R. James, (Oxford, 1924), pp. 94-146.
41. "Altenglische Legenden, neue Folge", ed. Hortsmann (Heilbvonn, 1881), p. 112.
42. Ed. E.-P. Migne, "Patrologia Latina", Vol. LXXXIII, col.

149.
43. Ed. Grasse (Leipzig, 1846)
44. It is important to realize that the inclusion of such stories as dealing with the childhood of Christ, the childhood of Our Lady and the "pound of flesh" incident in the story of the finding of the cross are embelishments to the "Cursor Mundi" as a whole. They add to the pleasure without detracting from the unity of the poem.
45. Hilda Graef, "Devotion to the Blessed Virgin" (London, 1963), p. 40.
46. "Cursor Mundi", G. II. 108-110.
47. "Cursor Mundi", G. II. 216-220.

Chapter II: Purpose of the Poem

1. "Cursor Mundi", G. II. 2-24
2. Jean Bodel, a French poet who flourished about 1200, was the first to divide the romances into three basic groups: the Matter of France, the Matter of Britain and the Matter of Rome the Great. In his "Chanson des Saxons", occur the often quoted lines: "ne sont que iii matieres a nul homme attendant,/De France et Bretagne et de Rome la grant." See "The Oxford Companion to French Literature", edd. Paul Harvey and J.E. Heseltine (Oxford, 1959), p. 75.
3. In its earlier form, it was not connected with the Arthurian cycle.
4. This is a popular "román d'aventure" of the first half of the 13th century. It is the story of the trials and success of a squire of low degree.
5. "Cursor Mundi", G. II. 25-26.
6. "Cursor Mundi", G. II. 45-62
7. "Cursor Mundi". G. II. 69-80.
8. "Cursor Mundi". G. II. 89-92.
9. "Cursor Mundi", G. II. 95-100.
10. "Cursor Mundi", G. II. 108-130.
11. "Cursor Mundi", G. II. 131-135.
    (It is significant that in this outline of the work, the "Cursor" poet does not mention that he will deal with the Oil of Mercy of the history of the Rood-tree. As a result, some critics say that all the section on the wandes which became the Cross are interpolated. A study of the text does not support this position.
12. "Cursor Mundi". G. II. 135-150.
13. "Cursor Mundi". G. II. 151-166
14. "Cursor Mundi". G. II. 167-192.
15. "Cursor Mundi". G. II. 197-202.
16. "Cursor Mundi". G. II. 213-215.

17. "Cursor Mundi". G. II. 219-220.
18. "Cursor Mundi". G. II. 225-230.
19. "Cursor Mundi". G. II. 267-270.
20. Bernard Ten Brink, "History of English Literature",Vol. 1, (New York, 1889) p. 288.
21. J. Murray, "Le Chateau d'Amour by R. Grosseteste" (Paris, 1918), vv. 1-7. (Who thinks well can say well; you cannot adequately begin any good undertaking without thought; may God grant us to think of Him, of whom, by whom, in whom are to be found all the good things that are in the world.)
22. J. Murray, 11-15 ss.
(We all have need of aid, but assuredly we cannot all know the languages of Hebrew, Greek, and Latin, to praise one's creator. So that the mouth of the singer may be unstopped to praise God and proclaim His holy name, and so that each one may know in his own tongue within himself without folly his God and his redemption, I begin my argument in French, for those who have neither letters or learning.)
23. "Sir Gawain and the Green Knight", ed. Isreal Gollanz, EETS os 210 (London, 1940 for 1937), pp. 1-18.
24. See "Cursor Mundi", G. I. 11797 f.
25. See the debate of Christ with the Doctors in the Temple in "Ludus Conventriae".
26. The wonders of Christ's childhood for example had been an accepted part of the oral tradition of the church for centuries and can be seen in stained glass windows and wall paintings in Medieval churches, 212

Chapter III: The Use of Prophecy as a Unifying Force

1. "Cursor Mundi", G. II. 1602-10
2. "Cursor Mundi", G. II. 6863-66.
3. Old Testament prophecies quoted by Chrust are too numerous to quote.
4. See Appendix "A" where some of the figures and fulfulments are indicated by square brackets. For example: the sacrifice of Isaac is a foreshadowing of the Crucifixion. See Kolve p. 72.
5. See "The Prophet's Play" in "The Chester Plays", ed. H. Deimling. EETS. es. 62, Part I (London, 1892), pp. 84-104.
6. "Cursor Mundi", G. II. 9265-68.
7. "Cursor Mundi", G. II. 9281-86.
8. "Cursor Mundi", G. II. 9287-88.
9. "Cursor Mundi", G. II. 9269 ff.
10. "Cursor Mundi", G. II. 9308-19.
11. "Cursor Mundi", G. II. 9337-44.
12. "Cursor Mundi", G. II. 9349-51.
13. "Cursor Mundi", G. II. 9355-64.
14. See "Cursor Mundi", G. II. 11361-72.
15. Ed. William C. Greet. EETS. os 171 (London, 1927), 71. (The object of this work, ca. 1456, is 'to win the lay children of the Church into obbediance' by rational arguments.)
16. Ibid., p. 71.
17. For a full explanation of Auerbach's arguments, see "Scenes from the Drama of European Literature", (New York, 1959), p. 188.
18. Louis Rean, "Iconographie de l'Art Chretian", (Paris, 1955-9), I. 192.
19. See "Romans", 5:15.
20. See Kolve, pp. 57-100.
21. "Cursor Mundi", G. II. 945-56.

22. Matthew 24:35-39.
23. "City of God", XV, 26.
24. "Cursor Mundi", G. I. 1761 ff.
25. "Mirk's Festial", pp. 77-78. (Sermon for Quinquagesima Sunday).

Chapter IV: The Use of Myth and Legend

1. E.M.W. Tillyrand, "Some Mythiical Elements in English Literature", (London, 1961), p. 10.
2. The Gnostics endeavored to create a Christianity which, fitting into the culture of the time would absorb the religious myths pf the Oriet and give the dominant role to the religious philosophy of the Greeks. They Tended to leave but a small place for revelation as the foundation of all theological knowledge, for faith, and for the Gospel of Christ. See Johannes Quasten, "Patrology", Vol. I, (Utrecht, 1966), pp. 154-78.
3. See "City of God", p. 204.
4. See Quasten, op. cit., p. 106.
5. "The Apocryphal New Testament", ed. M.R. James, (Oxford, 1924), pp. xi-xiii.
6. "The Apocryphal and Pseudepigrapha of the Old Testament", ed. Charles, II, 123-54. "The Apocalypse of Moses", written by an Alexandrian Jew in the first century A.D., belongs to a body of extracanonical literature which developed about Old Testament figures in the centuries before and after the Coming of Christ. See Robert Pfeiffer, "History of New Testament Times", (New York, 1949), p. 72.
7. Esther Casier Quinn, "The Quest of Seth", (Chicago, ill., 1962), p. 4.
8. Manderville, "Travels", I, 6-7.
9. Caxton, "The Golden Legend", I, 180, 111, 169.
10. Malory, "Works", II, 990-94.
11. Gayley, "Plays of Our Forefathers", pp. 246-71; Meyer, "Die Geschichte", pp. 155, 160.
12. "Ancient Cornish Drama", ed. and trans. Norris, I, 52-67, 131-43, 147-217, and cf. 425-27; see also "The Lengend of the Rood", trans. Halliday.
13. "Legends of the Holy Cross", ed. Morris, pp. 18-46, 19-

47, 62-96.

"Canticum de Creatione", in "The South English Legendary", edd. D.Evelyn and Mill, EETS os 235 (London, 1956), 167-74.

See also the version in "The Northern Passion" (Supplement), edd. Henser and Foster, EETS 183 (London, 1930). 31-34, 95-116.

14. William Wood Seymour, "The Cross in Tradition History and Art" (New York, 1898), p. 96.
15. Raimond Van Marle, "The Development of the Italian Schools of Painting" (The Hague, 1924) iii, 539 ff.
16. Roberto Longhi, "Piero della Francesca" (Milan, 1942), Plates XLIII-LXXX.
17. Seymour, p. 96.
18. John Ashton, "The Legendary History of the Cross", (New York, 1887), pp. CI-CLXXXVI.
19. See Wilhem Meyer, "Vitae adae et Evae".
20. This text seems to have been derived from a Greek translation of a lost Aramaic original.
21. Our summary is based on the translation of a text derived from MSS. "C" and "D" in Charles (ed.), "The Apocrypha and Pseudopigraphia of the Old Testament", II. 123-54.
22. William Meyer, "Die Geschichte", p. 207.
23. "The Apocryphal New Testament", ed. M.R. James, pp. 94-128.
24. Ed. Hulme, EETS 100 (London, 1907_
25. See William Meyer, op. cit., p. 108.
26. Meyer, op. cit., p. 131.
27. See Quinn, op cit., pp. 11-12.
28. See J.E. Cirlot, "A Dictionary of Symbols", (London, 1962), p. 70.
29. Edited at University of Greifswald, 1914, as a series of dissertations.
30. "Cursor Mundi", G. II. 945-956.

31. See St. Augustine, "City of God", XV, pp. 77, which deals with the meaning of the word "year" in the Book og Genesis and the possibility that it might be equivalent to the modern month because no early Old Testament figure has a child before he is 180 years of age.
32. "Cursor Mundi", G. II. 1283-1302.
33. "Cursor Mundi", G. II. 1267-88.
34. "Legend of the Holy Rood", ed. Richard Morris, p. 65.
35. "Cursor Mundi", G. II.1283-1302.
36. "Cursor Mundi", G. II. 1333-50.
37. "Cursor Mundi", G. II. 1355-62.
38. "Cursor Mundi", G. II. 1365-77.
39. "Cursor Mundi", G. II. 1377-86.
40. "Cursor Mundi", G. II. 1417-29.
41. "Cursor Mundi", G. II. 1431-32.
42. See: "History of the Holy Rood Tree", ed. A.S. Napier, EETS 103 (London, 1894) 2-35 MS Bodley 343 (formerly NE. F. 4. 12)
43. Ibid., p. 3.
44. Ibid., p. XII. Napier makes a thorough study of the various versions of this legend, which include "The Cambridge and Harleian Latin prose versions"; "The Andruis Fragments"; "Dboecvan den houte and Low German translations"; and "The Old French Poem". See 'Introduction', "History of the Holy Rood-Tree", pp. IX-LIX.
45. "Cursor Mundi", G. II. 6316-26.
46. "Cursor Mundi", G. II. 127-29.
47. "Cursor Mundi", G. II. 303-308.
48. "Cursor Mundi", G. II. 6339-46.
49. "Cursor Mundi", G. II. 6347-54.
50. "Cursor Mundi", G. II. 6365-68.
51. "Cursor Mundi", G. II. 6392-94.
52. "Cursor Mundi", G. II. 6664-66.
53. "Cursor Mundi", G. II. 6937-46.

54. "Cursor Mundi", G. II. 7973-8976.
55. "Cursor Mundi", G. II. 8005-08.
56. "Cursor Mundi", G. II. 8011-19.
57. "Cursor Mundi", G. II. 8041-50.
58. "Cursor Mundi", G. II. 8072-87.
59. "Cursor Mundi", G. II. 8099-8100.
60. "Cursor Mundi", G. II. 8111-14.
61. "Cursor Mundi", G. II. 8185-93.
62. "Cursor Mundi", G. II. 8203-20.
63. "Cursor Mundi", G. II. 8241-48.
64. "Cursor Mundi", G. II. 8837-42.
65. "Cursor Mundi", G. II. 8263-82.
66. "Cursor Mundi", G. II. 8521-31.
67. "Cursor Mundi", G. II. 8435-40.
68. "Cursor Mundi", G. II. 8451-76.
69. "Cursor Mundi", G. II. 8495-8508.
70. "Cursor Mundi", G. II. 8485-94.
71. "Cursor Mundi", G. II. 8766-70.
72. "Ecclesiastical History", IV, 6.
73. See the "Apocryphal New Testament", ed. M.R. James, pp. 49-65.
74. "Cursor Mundi", G. I. 12385 ff.
75. "Cursor Mundi", G. II. 8845-48.
76. "Cursor Mundi", G. II. 8867-74.
77. "Cursor Mundi", G. II. 8875-79.
78. "Cursor Mundi", G. II. 8905-08.
79. "Cursor Mundi", G. II. 8917-24.
80. "Cursor Mundi", G. I. 8928.
81. See John, V, 1-16 and also "Cursor Mundi", G. II. 13760-71.
82. A pool called 'Siloe' is mentioned in John, 9:7-11.
83. Meyer, "Die Geschichte", pp. 115-16.
84. "Cursor Mundi", G. II. 8939-42.
85. The Sibyl in several of the Middle English is confused with te Queen of Sheba. See "Legends of the Holy

Rood", p. xviii.
86. This is one of the few times that the 'Cursor' poet is confused with his Chronology. In line 8871, he says "after Solomon's day;" but in line 8956, he has the Sibyl coming to visit Solomon. The reason for this inconsistency may be due to the poet using several sources at the same time.
87. "Cursor Mundi", G. II. 8958-68.
88. "Cursor Mundi", G. II. 8974-76.

Chapter V: Climax in the Crucifixion

1. Walter Dukeshott, "The Sequence of English Medieval Art" (London, 1950), p. 20; see also "Early Medieval Illumination" intro. Hans. Swarenzenski (New York, 1951), PL. XV.
2. See Kolve, p. 175.
3. "The Northern Passion" (Supplement), p. 77, (1029-32).
4. "Cursor Mundi", G. II. 16615-28.
5. "Cursor Mundi", G. II. 16629-30.
6. "Cursor Mundi", G. II. 16713-14.
7. "Cursor Mundi", G. II. 16715-16.
8. "Inquiry into the Sources of the 'Cursor Mundi'" EETS 99 (London, 1892), p. 38.
9. "Cursor Mundi", G. II. 15961-64.
10. "Cursor Mundi", G. II. 15977-82.
11. "Cursor Mundi", G. II. 15983-98.
12. "The Northern Passion" (Supplement), pp. 116-117, (II. 2547-2604).
13. "The Northern Passion" (Supplement), II. 2603-04.
14. The beginning of the first Harmony of the Gospels goes back to Tatian, who about A.D. 175 combined in his Diatessaron the four Gospels into one continuous narrative, probably first in Greek; see "Dictionary of the Bible", ed. James Hastings (New York, 1963), p. 365.
15. Matthew XXVII: 3-5; Acts of Apostles. I:18.
16. "Cursor Mundi", G. II. 16501-04 and 16509-14.
17. The source for this is "The Story of the Holy Rood", in "Legends of the Holy Rood", ed. Morris, EETS 94, item no. 3 (London, 1871).
18. "Cursor Mundi", G. II. 16543-58.
19. "Cursor Mundi", G. II. 16581-93.
20. 'Oxford MS Rawlins on Poetry 175', "The Northern Passion" (Supplement), pp. 94-116 (II. 1748-2546).

21. "Cursor Mundi", G. II. 16599-16600.
22. "Northern Passion", II. 790-93.
23. Mark, XV:21.
24. "Cursor Mundi", G. II. 16683-90.
25. The English have always exhibited great interest in Pilate and his soldiers. A legend is that the Roman legion serving in Palestine at the time of the Crucifixion of Christ in Northern Gaul and Britian. The Royal Scots (the First of Foot), which is the oldest British regiment of the line, claims to be descended from Pontius Pilate's soldiers. The regiment nickname is 'Pontius Pilate's Bodyguard'. Another legend, used by dramatist James Bridie, says that Pilate was born in Scotland. The popular 'Punch and Judy' show is believed to have its origin in an Italian mystery play dealing with the Crucifixion. The various characters represent figures from the Passion.
26. "Cursor Mundi", G. II. 16665-80.
27. "Cursor Mundi", G. II. 16695-98.
28. Luke, XXIII:34.
29. "Stanzaic Life of Christ", p. 186 (II. 5541-48).
30. "Cursor Mundi", G. II. 16738-39.
31. Ch. X "...Dismas on His right hand, and Gesmas on the left, " "The Apocryphal New Testament". p. 174.
32. "Cursor Mundi", G. II. 16723-32.
33. "Cursor Mundi", G. II. 16734-36.
34. 'The Arabic Gospels of the Infancy', ub "The Apocryphal New Testament, ed. M.R. James, p. 81, (Chapter XXIII).
35. "Cursor Mundi", G. II. 16757-60.
36. "Cursor Mundi", G. II. 16777-78.
37. "Cursor Mundi", G. II. 16823-24.
38. "Cursor Mundi", G. II. 16829-30.
39. "Cursor Mundi", G. II. 16831-34.
40. John, 19:34.
41. Haenisch ("Inquiry into sources of the 'Cursor Mundi'"

p. 38), believes that the 'Cursor' poet got some of his details from Peter Comestor, "Historia Scholastica", p. 1634A.
42. "Cursor Mundi", G. II. 16835 ff.
43. "Cursor Mundi", G. II. 16845-48.
44. "Cursor Mundi", G. II. 16859-68. (This passage is found only in the Göttingen and Cotton MSS).
45. "Cursor Mundi", G. II. 16879-80.
46. "Cursor Mundi", G. II. 16913-22.
47. "Cursor Mundi", G. II. 16923-28.
48. "Cursor Mundi", G. II. 16939-44.

Chapter VI: The Harrowing of Hell

1. Oil is the symbol of the Grace of God. It is used in the sacraments of baptism, confirmation, ordination and unction.
2. "The Gospel of Nicodemus" in "The Apocryphal New Testament", ed. M.R. James, pp. 94-116.
3. See "The Apocryphal New Testament", pp. 132-34.
4. See Tillyard, pp. 20-21
5. "The Apocryphal New Testament", pp. 132-34.
6. "The Exultet Rolls", ed. Myrtilla Avery, (Princeton University Press, 1960)
7. See "The Blicking Homilies" ed. Morris, p. 85 ff; and also "The Homilies of the Anglo-Saxon Church", ed. Thorpe, 1, 26-38, 94, 108, 216, 218, 228, 248, 460; 11, 80, 606-608. The Anglo-Saxon text of the "Gospel of Nicodmus" has been edited by S.J. Crawford for the Awle Pyale Series (Edinburgh, 1927).
8. "Cursor Mundi", G. II. 17287-88.
9. The original manuscript (which is not in existence at the present day) could hardly have been written later than the middle of the 13th century. See "Middle English Harrowing of Hell and Gospel of Nicodemus", ed. Hulme, EETS, ES 100 (London, 1907).
   See also Ten Brink, op. cit., II, 241 ff.
10. "Cursor Mundi", G. vv. 17289-308.
11. "The Apocryphal New Testament", p. 105.
12. "Cursor Mundi", G. II. 17309-574.
13. One of the long digressions in the "Cursor Mundi" is on the evils of old age in the episode dealing with Jacob and Esau.
    See "Cursor Mundi", G. II. 3559-93.
14. "Cursor Mundi", G. II. 17579-88.
15. See Matthew, XXVII:52-3
16. "Cursor Mundi", G. II. 17897-804.

17. "Cursor Mundi", G. II. 17805-08.
18. "Cursor Mundi", G. I. 17813.
19. "The Apocryphal New Testament", p. 121.
20. "Cursor Mundi", G. II. 17833-44.
21. "Cursor Mundi", G. II. 17849-62.
22. "Cursor Mundi", G. II. 17863-68.
23. "Cursor Mundi", G. II. 17874-76.
24. "The Apocryphal New Testament", p. 124.
25. "Cursor Mundi", G. II. 17879-84.
26. See Luke, II:25
27. "Cursor Mundi", G. II. 17888-96.
28. "Cursor Mundi", G. II. 17902-06.
29. "Cursor Mundi", G. II. 17919-24.
30. "Cursor Mundi", G. II. 17928-36.
31. "Cursor Mundi", G. II. 17957-71.
32. First printed by Rosemary Woolf, "The Theme of Christ the Lover-Knight in Medieval English Literature", RES XIII (1926), 12. She thinks the vernacular phrases in the sermon suggest an English version known to the author. (For a horse he had the cross upon which he hung; for a shield he offered his side, and he advanced against the enemy so, with a spear not in his hand but sticking in his isde.)
33. "Cursor Mundi", G. II. 17989-92.
34. "Cursor Mundi", G. I. 17994 and II. 18001-10.
35. "Cursor Mundi", G. II. 18039-44.
36. "Cursor Mundi", G. II. 18063-72.
37. The Mystery Cycle developed following the establishment of the Feast of Corpus Christi early in the 14th century.
38. "Cursor Mundi", G. II. 18077-78.
39. "Cursor Mundi", G. II. 18080-82.
40. "Cursor Mundi", G. II. 18095-97.
41. "Cursor Mundi", G. II. 18103-04.
42. "Cursor Mundi", G. II. 18135-48.

43. "Cursor Mundi", G. II. 18155-60.
44. See "Cursor Mundi", G. II. 18155-60.
45. "Cursor Mundi", G. II. 18202-212 and II. 18215-220.
46. "The Apocryphal New Testament", p. 136.
47. "Cursor Mundi", G. II. 18221-26.
48. See Woolf, "The Theme of Christ the Lover-Knight", pp. 1-3.
49. The daring innovation made by the author of "Piers Plowman" was to combine the theme of the Four Daughters of God, treated separately in the "Cursor Mundi" (ll. 9517-9812), with the Harrowing of Hell.
50. "Cursor Mundi", G. II. 18259-64.
51. "Cursor Mundi", G. II. 18293-300.
52. "Cursor Mundi", G. II. 18304-306.
53. "Cursor Mundi", G. II. 18321-36.
54. "Cursor Mundi", G. II. 18489-90.
55. Ephesians, IV:9.
56. Phil., II:10.
57. Introduction', "The Middle English Harrowing of Hell and Gospel of Nicodemus", p. LXII.
58. "Cursor Mundi", G. II. 18643-54.

Chapter VII: The Finding of the Cross

1. See "The Catholic Encyclopedia", ed. Charles Herbermann, vol. 4 (New York, 1908), p. 523 ff.
2. See "inquiry into the Sources of the 'Cursor Mundi'", p. 56.
3. See "Butler's Lives of the Saints", ed. H. Thurston, S.J., Vol. III (New York, 1962), p. 346.
4. "Cursor Mundi", G. II. 16913-22.
5. "Cursor Mundi", G. II. 16923-26.
6. "Cursor Mundi", G. II. 21347-48
7. "Cursor Mundi", G. II. 21375-76.
8. "Cursor Mundi", G. II. 21378-79.
9. This part of the "Cursor Mundi" (II. 21347-846) was published separately, from the Fairfax MS by Richard Morris in his "Legends of the Holy Rood", pp. 108-121.
10. "Cursor Mundi", G. II. 211-12.
11. "Cursor Mundi", G. II. 21394-96.
12. The forms of this name in the "Cursor Mundi" are interesting as they preserve the Old French difference between the cases, which the English author must have taken over unaltered from his last original. They are: 21413 "Ansiers", nom L: messagers, plural; 21443 Ansiers, nom (fers); 21475 Ansire, acc. (ire).
13. "Cursor Mundi", G. II. 21451-54.
14. See "The Catholic Encyclopedia", Vol. 8, 773.
15. "Cursor Mundi", G. II. 21525-26.
16. "Cursor Mundi", G. II. 21534-36.
17. "Cursor Mundi", G. II. 21553-60.
18. "Cursor Mundi", G. II. 21627-28.
19. "Cursor Mundi", G. II. 21631-34.
20. "Cursor Mundi", G. II. 21649-56.
21. "Cursor Mundi", G. II. 21657-62.
22. "Cursor Mundi", G. II. 21663-68.
23. "Cursor Mundi", G. II. 21719-26.

24. "Cursor Mundi", G. II. 21733-40.
25. P. Didron, "Histoire de Dieu", (Paris, 1843), p. 351.
26. A nodern English translation of this work is in R. K. Gordon's "Anglo Saxon Poetry" (London, 1916), pp. 235-39. It is found in the Vercelli MS and part of it is inscribed in runes on the Ruthwell Cross in Annandale, Scotland.
27. "Cusor Mundi", G. II. 21801-08.
28. See "The Catholic Encyclopedia", Vol. IV, 517-28.
29. Anna Brownell (Murphy) Jameson, "Legends of the Monastic Orders" (Boston, 1901), p. 70. (The remark on "Pilgrim's Progress" is not so true in the mid-20th century as when Mrs. Jameson wrote it in 1848).
30. See for additional information Anna Jameson, p. 71.
31. Pope John XXIII dropped this feast from the Roman Calendar in July, 1966.
32. The popular animosity against the Jews on the charge of usury and the use of Christian blood at their Passover was general across western Europe at the time of the writing of the "Cursor MundI". This was in spite of the papal bull, issued by Gregory X in 1273, ordaining that no injury be inflicted upon any Jew or his property. Church authorities often were unable to restrain the people from massacring the Jews.
33. "Butler's Lives of the Saints", p. 229.
34. "Cursor Mundi", G. II. 21834-36.
35. "Cursor Mundi", G. II. 21837-46.

Chapter VIII: Recognition of Our Lady's Role in the History of Salvation

1. See "Cursor Mundi", G. II. 24764-24968, which ends the poem proper. The Cotton, Fairfax and Göttingen MSS contains additional poems including an exposition of the Apostle's Creed, and expplation of the Lord's Prayer, a prayer to the Trinity and a Book on Penance. These poems may quite possibly have been written by the "Cursor" poet, but are outside the scope of this work.
2. "Cursor Mundi", G. II. 219-220.
3. "Cursor Mundi", G. II. 111-120.
4. "Cursor Mundi", G. II. 121-123.
5. See Hilda Graef, "Devotion to the Blessed Virgin", (London, 1963), pp. 38-63.
6. Henry Adama, "Mont-Saint-Michel and Chartres", (New York, 1913), pp. 38-63.
7. Henry Adams pp. 100-101.
8. See "Cursor Mundi", G. I. 7014.
9. See "Cursor Mundi", G. I. 7048.
10. See "Cursor Mundi", G. II. 7056-62.
11. "Cursor Mundi", G. II. 7995-8036.
12. "Cursor Mundi", G. II. 16753-62.
13. "Cursor Mundi", G. II. 16879-80.
14. Francis X. Weiser. "Handbook of Christian Feast and Customs", (New York, 1952), p. 38.
15. "Cursor Mundi", G. II. 16923-26.
16. "Cursor Mundi", G. II. 17067-78.
17. "Cursor Mundi", G. II. 20015-20.
18. "Cursor Mundi", G. II. 20043-56.
19. Edmund, Archbishop of Canterbury from 1234 to his death in exile six years later, was one of the most learned men of his age. His pupils included Robert Grossetest**é and Roger Bacon.**

20. "Cursor Mundi", G. II. 20061-64.
21. Ed. Lumby, EETS os 14 (London, 1866), p. 75. The legend of the Assumption of our Lady had wide circulation in the Middle Ages. The "Cursor" poet may have also used Wace's version in his "Conception Notre Dame".
22. "Cursor Mundi", G. II. 20153-54.
23. "Cursor Mundi", G. II. 20213-14.
24. "Cursor Mundi", G. II. 20601-04.
25. "Cursor Mundi", G. II. 20799-802.
26. The "Cursor" poet's preoccupation with careful riming is expressed in the following:
Abiud yeit cam of him,
Of Abiud, Elyachim,
Of quan asor, sadoch of him
Þat loth er for to lig in rim.

("Cursor Mundi", G. II. 9237-40.)
27. "Cursor Mundi", G. II. 23909-12.
28. For Braswell's argument see "The Southern English Legendary Collection: a study in Middle English Religious Literature of the 13 and 14th centuries". (Unpublished Ph.D. Dissertation, University of Toronto, 1964), p. 415.
29. "Cursor Mundi", G. II. 23945-24658.
30. This rhyme scheme is AABCCB.
31. "Cursor Mundi", G. II. 24077-82.
32. "Cursor Mundi", G. II. 24635-40.
33. "Cursor Mundi", G. II. 24734-38.
34. See note 7 of Introduction for the significance of this disrespectful reference to an English king.
35. "Cursor Mundi", G. II. 24765-74.
36. "Cursor Mundi", G. II. 24774-84.
37. "Cursor Mundi", G. II. 24785-96.
38. "Cursor Mundi", G. II. 24800-02 and I. 24806.

39. "Cursor Mundi", G. II. 24821-26.
40. It is worth noting that the "Cursor" poet take one hundred lines to describe the background of the Abbot's journey. In most versions, this is done in a few sentences. For example, this is how Mirk introduces the legend:

> But now shull ye here how Þys fest war fouden. Þer was yon England a Kyng, was clept Wylliam Þe Conquerour Þat send Þe abbot of Ramsey to Þe Kyng of Denmark on message. But when he was in Þe see, Þer com a derkenesse to hym...

(Mirk's Festial, p. 17.)
41. "Cursor Mundi", G. II. 24837-44.
42. "Cursor Mundi", G. II. 24845-52.
43. "Cursor Mundi", G. II. 24890-98 and 24901-04.
44. "Cursor Mundi", G. II. 24931-34.
45. "Cursor Mundi", G. II. 24962-68.

Selected Primary Source

"Cursor Mundi". Ed. Richard Morris. 6 vols. EETS. os. 57, 59, 62, 66, 68, 99. London, 1874-92.

Other Primary Sources

Aelfric of Winchester. "Lives of the Saints". Ed. Walter Skeat. EETS. es. 75, 82. London, 1851-85.

"Apocryphal New Testament, The." Ed. Montague Rodes James. London: Oxford University Press, 1953.

Augustine. "The City of God". Ed. V.J. Bourke. New York: Doubleday and Co. 1950.

"Blickling Homilies of the Tenth Century, The." Ed. Richard Morris. EETS. os. 73. London: Kelmscott Press, 1892.

Caxton, William. "The Golden Legend". London: Kelmscott Press, 1892.

"Chester Plays, The" Edd. Herman Deimling and J. Matthews. 2 vols. EETS. es. 62, 115. London, 1892-1916.

Comestor, Peter. "Historia scholastic". Ed. Migne, "Patrologia Latina", Vol. 198. Paris, 1840-1881.

"Early English Homilies". Ed. R. D-N. Warner. EETS. os. 152. London, 1917.

"Early English Homilies". Ed. R. D-N. Warner. EETS. os. 152. London, 1917.

"Early English Texts". Edd. B. Dickens and R.M. Wilson. Cambridge: Bowes and Bowes, 1952.

"Early South English Legendary, The." Ed. Carl Hortsmann. EETS. os. 87. London, 1887.

Herman. "Li livres de la Bible". Edd. par Mancel et Trebutien. Caen, 1842.

Higden, Ranulf. "Polycronicon". Ed. Churchill Babington. Rolls Series 41. London, 1865.

Honorius of Autun. "Opera Omnia". Ed. Migne. "Patrologia Latina", 172. Paris, 1895.

Jacopo de Voraigine. "Legenda aurea". Ed. T. Graesse. 2nd ed. Leipzig, 1850.

Jocelyn of Brakelond. "Chronica". Ed. Thomas Arnold in "Memorials of Saint Edmund's Abbey". Rolls Series, 96. London, 1890.

"Legends of the Holy Rood". Ed. Richard Morris. EETS. os. 46. London, 1871.

"Ludus Conventriae or the Plaie Called Corpus Christi". Ed. K.S. Block. EETS. es. 120. London, 1922.

"Middle English Harrowing of Hell and Gospel of Nicodemus, The" Ed. William Henry Hulme. EETS. es. 100. London, 1908.

"Mirk's Festial" Ed. Theodore Erbe. EETS. os. 29. London 1867.

"Norther Passion, The." Ed. Frances A. Foster. 2 vols. EETS. os. 145, 147. London, 1913-16.

"Norther Passion (Supplement), The." Edd. Wilhelm Heuser

and Frances A. Foster. EETS. os. 183. London, 1930.

"Old English Homilies" Ed. Richard Morris. EETS. os. 29. London 1867.

"Ormulum" Ed. Robert Holt. 2 vols. Oxford, 1878.

Pecock, Reginald. "Reule of Chrysten Religioun" Ed. William C. Greet. EETS. os. 171. London, 1927.

"Robert of Brunne's Handlyng of Synne" Ed. F.J. Furnivall. 2 vols. EETS. os. 119, 123. London, 1901.

"South English Legendary" Edd. Charlotte D'Evelyn and Anna Jean Mill. 2 vols. EETS. os. 235, 236. London, 1926.

"Speculum Sacerdotale" Ed. Edward H. Weatherly. EETS. os. 200. London, 1936.

"Stanzaic Life of Christ" Ed. Frances A. Foster. EETS. os. 166. London, 1926.

Selected Bibliography Secondary Sources

Adams, Henry. "Mont-Saint-Michel and Chartres" New York: Doubleday and Co., 1913.

Aitken, T.H. "Edude sur le Miroir de Robert Gretham" Paris, 1922.

Ashton, John. "The Legendary History of the Cross" New York, 1887.

Auerbach, Erich. "Scenes from the Drama of European Literature" New York: Macmillan and Co., 1959.

Barth, Curt. "Der Wortschatz des Cursor Murnk" Konigsberg Dissertation, 1903.

Beichner, P. "The Cursor Mundi and Petrus Riga", "Speculum", XXIV (1949), 239.

Bennet, J.A. W. (ed.) "Early Middle English Verse and Prose". London: Oxford Univeristy Press, 1914.

Borland, L. "Herman's Bible and the Cursor Mundi", XXX (1933), 427-497.

Braswell, Laurel. "The South English Legendary Collection." Unpublished dissertation, University of Toronto, 1964.

Chambers, R.W. "Continuity of English Prose from Alfred to More and his School" –Introduction to Nicholas Harpsfield's "Life of Sir Thomas More" London, 1932.

Charles, R.D. (ed.) "The Apocrypha and Pseudepigraphia of the Old Testament" London: Oxford University Press, 1913.

Collingwood, R.G. "The Idea of History" London: Macmillan and Co., 1946.

Craig, H. "English Religious Drama" London: Oxford University Press, 1955.

Danielou, Jean. "From Shadow to Reality" London: Longmans, 1966.

-----. "The Lord of History". London: Longmans, 1958.

Deansley, Margaret. "The Lollard Bible" Cambridge: University Press, 1920.

D'Evelyn, Charlotte. "Methodius as Source", PMLA XXII (1918), 147.

Gaffrey, Wilbur. "The Allegory of the Christ-Knight in 'Piers Plowman'", PMLA CLVI (1931), 158-60.

Gayley, Charles Mills. "Plays of Our Forefathers" New York: Macmillan and Co., 1907.

Gordon, R.K. (trans.) "Anglo Saxon Poetry" London: J.M. Dent and Sons, 1916.

Graef, Hilda. "Devotion to the Blessed Virgin" London: Burns and Oates, 1963.

Harvey, Paul, and Heseltine, J.E. (edd.) "The Oxford Companion to French Literature" London: Oxford University Press, 1959.

Hulme, W.H. "The Old English 'Gospel of Nicodemus'", PMLA XIII (1913), 457 ff.

Kaiser, Rolf. "Zur Geographie des mittelenglischen wortschatzes" Leipzig, 1937.

Kaluza, Max. "Zu den Quellen und den HSS—Verhaltnis des 'Cursor Mundi'", "Englische Studien", Vol. XII (1888)

Kington, Oliphant, T.L. "The Old and Middle English" London, 1878.

Kolve, V.A. "The Play Called Corpus Christi" Stanford University Press, 1966.

Lamberts, Jacob J. "The Dialect of Cursor Mundi" (Cotton MS Vespasian A III). Unpublished Dissertation, University of Michigan, 1954.

Legge, M.D. "Anglo-Norman in the Cloisters" Edinburgh: Edinburgh University Press, 1950.

Meyer, Wilhelm. "Die Geschichte des Kreuzholzes vor Christus", "Abhandlungen der philosophisch-philologischen Classe der Koniglich Baverischen Classe der Koniglich Baverischen Akademie der Wissenschaften" (Munich) XVI (1879), 187-250.

Murray, James A.H. "The Dialect of the Southern Counties of Scotland" London 1873.

Quasten, Johannes. "Patrology" Utrecht: Spectrum Publishers, 1966.

Quinn, Esther Casier. "The Quest of Seth". Chicago: University of Chicage Press, 1962.

Schipper, Jakob. "Altenglische Metrik" Bonn, 1881.

Strandberg, Otto. "The Rime-Vowels of Cursor Mundi" Upsalla Dissertation, 1919.

Ten Brink, Bernard. "The History of English Literature" New York: Henry Holt and Co., 1889.

Tillyard, E. M. W. "Some Mythical Elements in English Literature". London: Chatto and Windus, 1961.

Weiser, Francis X. "The South English Legendary in its relation to the 'Legenda aurea'", PMLA LI (1936), 337-60.

Acknowledgements

Acknowledgement is gratefully made to Dr. Hudson, the Early English Text Society and Miss Raybould of Oxford University Press for their extreme helpfulness in making availiable the original text from their edition of the "Cursor Mundi".

Chapter VIII of this study appeared in a slightly altered version in "Revue de l'Universite d'Ottawa" (Juillet-Septembre 1968); and the chapter dealing with the finding of the Cross was first printed, again slightly altered, in "Eglise et Theologie" (Winter 1969). A grateful thanks to the editors of these two Canadian periodicals for permission to reprint this material.

This work developed from a doctoral dissertion, accepted by the Unuversity of Ottawa. The assistance obtained from the University of Ottawa library staff is also acknowledged.

www.ingramcontent.com/pod-product-compliance
Lightning Source LLC
Chambersburg PA
CBHW022013300426
44117CB00005B/170